Cathy

My Very Best,

Al Trottis

Against the Odds

Leslie Trotter Zwingli and Lt.
Colonel Elmer John (Al) Trotter,
DFC,DFM,CD,CM (retired)

authorHOUSE®

AuthorHouse™
1663 Liberty Drive
Bloomington, IN 47403
www.authorhouse.com
Phone: 1-800-839-8640

First published by AuthorHouse   8/4/2009

ISBN: 978-1-4389-8633-3 (e)
ISBN: 978-1-4389-8631-9 (sc)
ISBN: 978-1-4389-8632-6 (hc)

Printed in the United States of America
Bloomington, Indiana

This book is printed on acid-free paper.

On the cover: Oil painting by Kamloops, B.C. artist, John Rutherford ,
depicting Al's Lancaster the early morning of December 3, 1943.

One of the lucky things about being a writer is that you get to meet interesting people and hear exciting stories. There can be few more exciting than the life story of one of Canada's truly great warriors – Elmer (Al) Trotter.

Al has been a fighter all his life. As a youngster, growing up in Tuberose Saskatchewan, he was often in trouble, not intentionally so, but never inclined to back down. Then with war looming, a decision to join the air force meant the constant challenge of training both at home, and later in England, where again his culture clashed both literally and metaphorically with his new-found 'allies'.

He persevered, however, and after nearly two and half years of training through the usual pattern of flying training schools, operational training units, and conversion units he went from single-engine through to twin-engine and then four-engine aircraft before finally qualifying as a pilot in charge of his own aircraft and crew, flying the legendary Lancaster.

Posted to 101 (Special Duties) Squadron at Ludford Magna, Al soon found himself in the thick of the action, flying his first operation to Berlin, to the very heart of Nazi Germany. His squadron's aircraft flew with a secret 'eighth man' who operated a similarly secret transmitter to jam signals from Luftwaffe night fighter controllers. So essential were these crews that they flew on every major bomber command operation, and so took the highest casualties. Elmer and his crew very nearly added to this statistic when on only their fourth operation they were intercepted by a night fighter and badly shot up. Through a combination of skill and determination the crew managed to make it home in one piece, and Elmer was awarded a well-earned Distinguished Flying Medal for his courage. It was not the only time he would display such fortitude in the face of adversity, or be rewarded for his bravery.

Shortly after, Al was recommended by his commanding officer to join an even more hazardous outfit, the Pathfinders, described as the elite of bomber command, and for very good reason. The pathfinders flew at the vanguard of every mission, finding and marking the target for the following 'main force' to bomb. Posted first to 156 Squadron at RAF Warboys, Al began to experience the real horror of war first hand, flying a succession of long and dangerous operations over the night skies of Germany and beyond, with flights of more than nine hours being not uncommon – nine hours with the thought (and threat) that any minute they might become the victim of flak or fighters.

Whilst many of his comrades fell, some never to return, Elmer and his crew survived, even the disastrous night of March 30th 1944 when bomber command suffered its highest losses of the war. Posted again to 582 Squadron in Little Staughton, Bedfordshire, Al's luck finally ran out on his 44th operation. His gunners failed to spot a night fighter lurking in the gloom on the way back from Russelsheim, and they were shot down, four of his crew being killed. Elmer survived – again – despite taking to his 'chute late and with his aircraft perhaps only 500ft above the ground. Making a run for it, he was quickly captured and taken for interrogation. Constantly threatened with execution both as a 'Terrorflieger' and a spy, it was with relief that he was eventually sent to prison camp, and the infamous Stalag Luft III, where yet another horror was about to unfold.

Al's story is relentless in its action, made more exciting by its simple telling. This is not a book that needs hyperbole; the drama is there in his own words. His descriptions of everyday (and some not so 'everyday!') events, made more interesting by their historical context, are particularly engaging: his friendships; the obvious respect for his 'adoptive' father and the support of his parents; the excitement of the visit of the King, Queen Elizabeth and Princess Elizabeth to his squadron to the point that he couldn't eat.

Then his descriptions when staring danger and possible death in the face – not just once but on several occasions: on the boat coming over from Canada to England when they were attacked by a U-boat; his fight with the Black Watch and his 'dumb farm boy trick' of never walking away; his description of bailing out, and being bounced around the cockpit like a tennis ball; of being blindfolded, and facing a firing squad. Of the death march.

Al's experiences were perhaps more exciting than many, but he doesn't claim to be any more special; far from it. And that is what makes this story so good. Whereas it helps, perhaps, to have a wider understanding of the role of bomber command in the Second World War, and Pathfinders specifically, that does not detract from what is still an exciting tale that anyone can enjoy. His view through his writing and Leslie's telling of his story is understated, and more powerful because of it. He was a survivor. Against the odds.

Sean Feast
Sarratt, England, November 2008
Author of Carried on the Wind, Heroic Endeavour and Master Bombers, and A Pathfinder's Story

I started reading your father's book last night and couldn't stop until I had finished it. It is a charming story of the growth of a young Saskatchewan farm boy into a secure bomber pilot - leading his crew as "family." I was struck by the concern of his ground crew and again it spoke well of your father and his crew. What particularly interested me was his successful attempt to get in touch with his mother by extra-sensory perception when he was shot down.

Don Elliott (Pappy to the Kriegies)

In addition to recording the military exploits of a young, very brave Pathfinder bomber pilot during the Second World War, this down-to-earth, in-the-trenches (skies) recap of many harrowing brushes with the grim-reaper saga perpetuates the memory of those ten thousand heroic men and women of the Royal Canadian Air Force who gave their lives in Bomber Command.

Although a bit heavy with training and individual flight recollections, we move quite smoothly into heavy bomber operations (800-900 aircraft), heavy losses (up to 90 aircraft per sortie) and into the 44th and fatal mission (shot down by a night-fighter attack). Of note thereafter is the nearly nine months spent as a prisoner-of-war, culminating in the Horror March (eight days of wintertime pain and suffering barely endured by 250000 prisoners, of whom 25000 perished). Liberation: May 2nd, 1945.Unfortunately, although extremely interesting in scope and unabashed, almost total recall of personal details, it is a shame we didn't get this story twenty to thirty years ago so that more of our veterans could have shared in and truly empathized with Elmer J's incredible wartime experiences. All in all, very interesting reading, written by a loving daughter, as told by a caring and loving father. For me and others who have followed W/C Al's post-wartime career, this provides great insight into what made him the man that he was and remains. As they say in the military, Bravo Zulu!

Major Don Little, RCAF retired.

The very thought of doing your nursery as a raid on Berlin is shattering to say the least for anyone who has any knowledge of bomber operations. And to have your resolute and skillful airmanship rewarded by an offer to volunteer for Pathfinders is of questionable generosity!

Brigadier General Jack Watts RCAF retired
Former Squadron Commander 109 Squadron based along with 582 Squadron at Little Staughton

You and your Dad have hit a home run with this book in my eyes and I think it is one of the very best personal accounts I have ever read on the war. You had an incredible story to begin with and have done it justice with your writing. The story about the new arrivals at Stalag Luft III having nightmares and crying out "abandon aircraft" only takes a few lines yet tells so much about what frame of mind they and the men who baled from their bunks were in. I think the other thing that makes this book significant is the timing. Most of the books written by Bomber Command men came out in the 80's and 90's and have been dwindling as the men approached their 80s. This is one of the last that will be written and one of the best on the subject. Its strength is in its telling, free of any ego or self promotion. It is a great read and I look forward to having a finished copy on my bookshelf - hopefully autographed by you and your father.

Congratulations
Dave Wallace
Son of Flight Lieutenant Alexander Cameron Wallace, Oboe Navigator with Wing Commander Graham Foxall and crew, 109 Mosquito Squadron, Little Staughton

Foreword

By
Lieutenant-General Donald McNaughton, CMM, CD
(retired)
Former Commander of Air Command, Canadian Forces

After completing his pilot training, Elmer John (Al) Trotter, age 19, left for Europe in November 1942, to fight for his country in World War 2. He returned to Canada in June of 1945 at the end of the war, a decorated Air Force warrior who had been awarded both the Distinguished Flying Medal (DFM) and the Distinguished Flying Cross (DFC).

In his time in Europe Al Trotter piloted a Lancaster bomber and headed a crew of seven who took their war to the enemy at night. The environment that the crew operated within was absolutely daunting: heavy bomb loads, short runways, bad weather, flak, enemy night fighters, and a crowded airspace. In addition, most of Al's missions were as a pathfinder, the aircraft that marked the targets for the main bomber flow; this activity increased exposure to fire and the inherent danger of being shot down. It is said that only one activity in World War 2 was more dangerous than that of a bomber crew and that was as a crew on a German U-Boat!

Al Trotter defied the odds miraculously, dodging many bullets along the way. He was on his 44th mission over enemy territory on August 12th, 1944, when an unseen enemy fighter plane literally blew his Lancaster out of the sky. Al was able to bail out, was ultimately captured, and spent months in a Prisoner of War camp. Near the end of the war, his final trial was to survive the long march when POWs were moved westward.

I was privileged to work for Wing Commander Trotter for three years in the mid-sixties when he was Commanding Officer of a Flying Training School. He was probably the best boss I ever had, a superb officer and one who knew how to accomplish the mission.

Al always has a reticence to talk about his wartime experiences so we were certainly pleased to hear that he, along with his daughter Leslie, has written this book, which will record for posterity, the actions of this brave warrior who did indeed survive, "against the odds".

FOREWORD

In the early years of the war, RAF Bomber Command was the main, if not the only offensive of the Allied Forces. It was a valiant effort by the individual crews, ill equipped as they were and suffering heavy casualties. Despite being relatively ineffective on many occasions, the crews of Bomber Command returned night after night, despite their losses, determined to pursue their attacks and to limit Germany's ability to wage war.

It was in 1942 that the most significant step in making Bomber Command more effective was made – the formation of the Pathfinder Force (PFF). The crews of PFF were volunteer crews from within the Command who were already battle conditioned and recommended for their devotion to duty, their determination, their personal high standards and their proficiency, let alone extend their tour by 50% from 30 to 45 sorties. These crews would lead the Main Force to the target and keep the target marked with fluorescent markers throughout the raid. These crews set the standard and were the "Aces" of Bomber Command.

Lt. Colonel Trotter's story, Against the Odds, is a living testimony to this evolution in Bomber Command history. His story illustrates how a young Canadian matures during training to become a leader and captain of a multi-engine aircraft and crew on death defying raids. After demonstrating incredible airmanship and bringing his severely damaged aircraft and crew home after a successful raid in Germany, he not only continued to fly on his tour but volunteered for and was accepted by PFF where he continued to demonstrate all those admirable qualities which fitted him to be a Pathfinder.

Brigadier General J.V.Watts, DSO, DFC, CD Retired

Former Squadron Leader 109 Mosquito Squadron based at Little Staughton

INTRODUCTION

There are numerous statistics for review however; the generally accepted average life expectancy for bomber crews on their first tour of thirty operations is about six percent. That number dropped to between three and four percent for the crews of the Pathfinder forces who, before receiving credit for a double tour, were required to fly forty five trips.

Canada, with a total population of 11,381,000 in 1940, lost 55,000 young men during this war. The losses of the Royal Canadian Air Force was estimated at 17,000 and 10,000 were in Bomber Command alone.

This is the saga of one young Canadian pilot's story of survival from enlistment, through wartime operations, capture and imprisonment and participation in the horror/death march and finally repatriation.

He was one of only thirty seven members of the R.C.A.F. to receive both the Distinguished Flying Medal and the Distinguished Flying Cross during World War II and went on to serve in both the Korean War and the Cold War.

PREFACE

The writing of this story has been an incredible journey back in time to a period of our history generations of today and of the future must never forget. It has been a journey of love, admiration and deep respect for my father, who like, so many others, sacrificed his youth, innocence and in so many cases their lives, that we could enjoy the freedoms and opportunities we have today.

For my father, it has been a journey back to a time close to sixty seven years ago, sometimes recounting painful memories, and finally giving him some closure with respect to certain episodes, which had occurred.

As a child growing up, I would ask my father about his war experiences. He would usually tell little anecdotes that were humorous, and although he told of his being shot down and taken as a prisoner of war, he gave very few details of his wartime exploits.

I have been pressuring him for a number of years to write his memoirs, as I believed his experiences, should be recorded for history and for his grandchildren.

I believe it was near the end of his thirteen year battle with the Canadian Government over retroactive Prisoner of War Pensions, (which he won in the Supreme Court of Canada), where he had to recount his history several times before a panel of judges, he came to the realization that preservation of these stories was important. The telling of his story would help to ensure the memories of those who died, along with those who survived would not be forgotten. In addition, he said, "I began to realize I had cheated my children of knowledge of their father, and perhaps insight into events which had shaped the person their father was.

In September 2005, the year the Canadian Government had declared as "The Year of the Veteran" Dad and I began our amazing journey together.

DEDICATION

This book is dedicated to the memory of my Brothers in Arms, the crew of Lancaster ND969, 60"F" for Freddy.

Flight- Sergeant Kenneth Archibald, Rear Gunner, Pilot Officer Bernard Pullin, DFC (Posthumously), Bomb Aimer, Sergeant Walter Parfitt, Mid Upper Gunner, and Sergeant John Thomas Broad, Wireless Operator/Gunner, who were killed in action that fateful night of August 12/13, 1944.

Flight Sergeant John Rawcliffe, Flight Engineer and Squadron Leader Barcroft Melrose Mathers, DFC and Bar, Navigator, who both survived and along with me, became Prisoners of War.

The dedication is also to all those who served and continue to serve their countries for the preservation of Peace, Democracy and continued Freedom.

ACKNOWLEDGEMENTS

This story would have been incomplete without the support and help of the following people:

Dave Wallace whose father was with 109 Mosquito Squadron stationed at Little Staughton, the home base of 582 Squadron. Dave was the first to reply to my initial inquiry on the internet, and has been the provider of many details as well as information sources for my research.

Robin Riley, web-master of 156 Squadron, whose incredible research was instrumental in providing information about my father, his crew, and their missions. In addition, a huge thank you for publishing some of the details of my father's story, along with photographs on his website.

Dr. Theo Boiten, historian and author of the Nachtjagd War Diaries, who through his research was able to provide the name of the pilot who shot my father down, the location of the crash site and the pilot presumed to be the attacker on Dec. 2, 1943.

Sean Feast, author of Carried on the Wind, Heroic Endeavour, and Master Bombers for his support and editing of the manuscript. His suggestions and professional expertise were invaluable in making this story an acceptable work.

Marilyn Jeffers Walton, author of Rhapsody in Junk, the story of her father's wartime experience, for her introduction to Hanns Claudius Schaarf, son of Hanns Schaarf, the Master

Interrogator at Dulag Luft, along with her support and suggestions.

To David Layne, Hugh Halliday, Erich, John, Max, Larry, Linda, Amrit, John Neal and so many more who are members of the following forums: Your responses to my research questions, along with your continued support in the writing of this story made the journey easier.

Bombercrew.com
RAF Commands 1939-1945
World War II Forums
World War II Talk
Lancaster Archives

My good friend Diane Bennett for the hours she spent editing and making suggestions with respect to punctuation wording and spelling.

My niece Cassie, for taking the time out of her busy work schedule to format this manuscript into a form acceptable to the Publisher.

Richard for his continued patience, support, and my mother Val for allowing me to take up so much of Dad's time.

Most importantly, thank you Dad, for allowing me to explore the depths of your mind, bringing back some painful memories you had suppressed for so long. Without your perseverance, tenacity and memory, despite illness and age, this story would not have been told. I hope it has brought you some closure and peace of mind with the resolution of many unanswered questions. I love you.

CONTENTS

CHAPTER ONE
THE BEGINNING

I was born in Santa Cruz California on February 23, 1923. I remember my Aunt Louise telling me my birth father was a World War I veteran named Charles Joyner, who had enlisted and was, wounded severely, medically discharged, and re-enlisted twice more under similar circumstances. He served with the Princess Patricia Canadian Light Infantry, and was one of the Regiment's first officers. During his last tour, he was again, wounded severely and having been exposed to mustard gas and shrapnel, had a rather large metal plate implanted in his head. Doctors had prescribed various medications to combat the pain. This resulted in major personality changes, which adversely affected my mother, who, pregnant with me, moved to California to the home of her grandmother. I was three years old when my father died at the age of thirty-seven, a direct result of his many very serious wounds. Consequently, I never knew him or his family.

Interestingly, I was able to corroborate my knowledge of my father and his military career, when I took Rob and Joel, two of my grandsons, to the excellent Military Museum in Calgary, Alberta. There in its' archives, my father's service in WWI was recorded. It is ironic that in the years 1948, 49, and 50, when I was stationed in Edmonton Alberta with #435 Transport Squadron, I dropped hundreds of the Princess Patricia Canadian Light Infantry paratroops based in Calgary, not knowing my real father was one of the Regiment's original officers.

About this time, my mother returned to Moose Jaw, Saskatchewan, Canada, and needing to provide for herself and a small child, she applied for and was accepted as a housekeeper for a bachelor schoolteacher and farmer named Frank Alexander Trotter. After a time they married, and Frank became the only father I ever knew.

Over the next few years, my mother and Dad had three children, Jack, Louise, and Fred, and we became a very closely knitted family unit.

My life growing up was that of a typical Saskatchewan farm boy. We lived in the small town communities of Tuberose and Sanctuary, and our farm in each case, was about 5 miles away. I went to school, played hockey, baseball, curling, and was very active in track and field. In addition, I helped my dad on the farm as and when ever needed.

I graduated from high school in Tuberose, Saskatchewan in 1941, with a grade average of 85%. My highest marks were in Trigonometry (97%) and Physics (89%). These marks would later influence my acceptance into the pilot training program.

My mother and stepfather had spoken quite often about dad formally adopting me, however, dad in his wisdom always felt it should be my decision whether to take his name. When I was eighteen, Dad officially adopted me as Elmer John Trotter, thereby recognizing my own wish to take the name of the only man, I had ever known as Dad, and who had so lovingly raised me as his own son.

When the war broke out in 1939, I began to listen avidly at every opportunity to the only daily news source available,

KSL radio in Salt Lake City, Utah. Our only newspaper was a weekly called the Western Producer, which was more involved with farming in the Prairie Provinces, than with International affairs.

My interest in joining up came about indirectly and ironically through my mother. She had issued an open invitation to the Royal Air Force (RAF) student pilot trainees stationed at #32 Advanced Flying Training School, in Swift Current, Saskatchewan under the British Commonwealth Air Training Plan, to stay with us in Tuberose on their weekends off. Many took advantage of mom's offer. These young men in RAF blue barely over my age, maybe eighteen or nineteen years old, telling stories about flying really aroused my interest. I had wanted to enlist since I was seventeen, however, my dad was recovering from major surgery, and I was needed to operate the machinery necessary, to farm nearly one thousand acres of cropland.

I think I have always been a strong advocate of our great country. I am proud to be a Canadian, have always been proud and will never change. This in conjunction with the visits from the RAF students is what influenced my desire to enlist.

I approached my father and mother, and, knowing full well, what my mother would say, I did most of my talking with Dad. He told me this was a decision that only I could make, but he would be very proud if I joined the Air Force.

I wrote to the Recruiting Centre in Regina Saskatchewan to get some details, and they wrote back very quickly telling me all my options. I sent the forms back specifying that I would like to be a wireless air gunner (WAG), as that had been the first thing that impressed me. The enlistment office very quickly made a date for me to come down and speak to a recruiting officer. When I arrived for my appointment, the Recruiting Officer tried to talk me into being a pilot as I had my Senior Matriculation, (University Entrance Requirements) and I was highly qualified for pilot training, I told him no, I want to be a gunner, so they enlisted me as such.

When I came home, I told my mother I was a wireless air gunner (WAG) and she asked me "what did that mean?" I told her the basics, leaving out any of the hazards associated with the position. Unfortunately, (or fortunately), shortly thereafter we had a visit from a couple of the RAF boys, and when my mother told them I had enlisted as a wireless air gunner they exclaimed, "Oh my God! Don't let him join up as an air gunner, the tail and mid upper gunners are the first targets the enemy fighter pilots aim for." Well that caused all hell to break loose. Mom started in on me saying she was going to call the recruiting office and tell them I was underage. "I'll have it cancelled!" She said. In my father's presence I said, "Mom, if you have it cancelled, I'll just run away and join the army," and I left her with that threat. I did not realize at the time, that she could not legally prevent me from enlisting, as I was eighteen years old. My dad talked to her at great length, and said if this was what I wanted to do, then they should not interfere.

Well, I thought about the situation for quite awhile, and because I loved my mother very much, I seriously considered the fact she was not well, and constantly worrying about me could quite likely cause her death. I called the Recruiting Office in Regina, and asked them to change my enlistment from Wireless Air Gunner to Pilot. The recruiting officer was very receptive and said to come to Regina to re- enlist and so down I went and joined up again. My enlistment date was September 1, 1941, an auspicious date for me, as it was that date nine years later, when I would marry my sweetheart Val, my wife and companion for the last 59 years.

I returned home after enlisting to await call up. Dad was not a drinker but on the first Saturday after my return from Regina, he surprised me with "Would you like to go into Kyle (the closest town with a beer parlour) and have a beer with your Dad?" I was very surprised, but quite pleased at this, and I quickly agreed.

We sat at a table, enjoying our beers when a local coyote hunter came over and greeted dad with civility. Dad said to him quite proudly, "Elmer has just joined the Air Force." The hunter responded, "Air Force! Did he not have enough guts to join the Army?"

Now Dad was only five feet six inches tall, a slightly built teacher/farmer but a great athlete who had played championship soccer and baseball. Our confronter was well-built and about six feet tall. Never-the-less Dad leaped to his feet, and with one punch to the jaw dropped this six-footer to the floor. He got up with a very shocked look on his face, and Dad followed up with "Now get the hell out of here before I hit you again!"

I was quite surprised as my Dad very seldom if ever used profanity, and certainly was not a violent man. To say I was very, very proud of him, would certainly qualify as one of the under-statements of the century.

CHAPTER TWO
BASIC TRAINING

My first posting after enlistment was to the Manning Depot in Brandon, Manitoba. This was certainly, where my real military experience started. I was there for approximately two months, but it was a demanding two months with so much information to absorb in such a short time frame, and the results of the final examinations (simplistic) once again, are the deciding factor as to whether or not you continued on your new career. "Ever thus".

This was quite a new experience for this little farm boy from Saskatchewan, who really knew nothing about life beyond the farm, and had only spent a total of two years while going to school in the big city of Moose Jaw Saskatchewan. It was here that I told my buddies that my nickname was EL, which in no time became AL. I hated the name Elmer, which I associated with a cartoon in our weekly News Paper starring Elmer Tuggle. Each week the cartoon would either start or end with a rather over weight mama, standing on the front step of her house, screaming ELMERRRRR. Not a very good reason in my adult mind, however from a teenager's perspective absolutely, essential. From the date of change from Elmer to Al, I rarely heard the name Elmer until I returned on leave to my home turf of Tuberose.

The Manning Depot was certainly a strange new environment in many ways, starting with the fact that we were crowded in a very large building located on the city fair grounds. The building housed hundreds of new recruits, sharing double-decker bunks with no room partitions what so ever, literally NO privacy.

One day the training officers called for volunteers, someone who could operate a tractor. Well, I sure had lots of experience operating tractors on the farm, so my hand went up real quick, as did about a dozen others. They said okay and we stepped forward only to find that the job they had for us was with wheelbarrows, hauling dirt and pouring concrete foundations for new buildings. I never did see a tractor.

I held the rank of aircraftsman second class, the lowest rank in the Canadian Air Force. The next rank was aircraftsman first class and that was the only one I missed in all my promotions.

They made me an acting Corporal at Manning Depot and my job was to meet the trains arriving with new recruits, and then march them out to the Manning Depot. "Mr. Big Shot" acting Corporal, unpaid I might add.

Never-the less, there were some amusing stories that came out of our first military posting. One that I will never forget occurred at 5.00AM with the arrival each morning, of the Sergeant Major bellowing out one of his favourite expressions, "let go of your cocks and grab your socks". We were scared of him, there was no doubt he was a mean son of gun as far as we were concerned, but it was seemingly an accepted part of our training.

This institution was also, where we had our first introduction to Parades. This meant lining up in military inspection style. We had parades from morning to sundown (to ensure you had not decided to terminate your new career). Meal parades, church parades, clothing parades (everything from your shoes up, if you got lucky everything would fit more or less). There were pay parades, oh boy a $ 1.30 per day paid every two weeks. Needle parades required lining up in alphabetical order and on command march forward, making sure you passed through the double line of doctors and/or nurses or medical aides. How do you tell who is who? In any event, it appeared to us sprogs (slang for new comers), that they were possibly new recruits like ourselves. There were also times when you could not help believing that they were not medical people, but just dart players practicing for an upcoming tournament. Another most embarrassing inspection was the "short arm," and I will leave that to your imagination.

Another experience I had at the Manning Depot, involved participating in the Friday night boxing card. If you took part, you would box on the Friday card and your reward would be a forty- eight hour pass the following weekend. Now I grew up in a family with a father who strongly believed the ability to hold your own in a rough and tough world was essential. Dad taught us boys the basic rudiments and skills necessary to defend ourselves, and whenever possible, entered my brother Jack and/or me in the few boxing card opportunities that came up every year in the larger towns. Jack, some seven or eight years later knocked out the Welter Weight Champion of Saskatchewan. Not bad for a young farmer.

I did quite well in my first couple of fights, but in my third, my adversary was a no show. The organizers at the last minute substituted another volunteer who was at least one if not two weight classes higher than I was. To make a long story short, I was the recipient of two black eyes, a cut eyebrow, and other facial wounds. He did such a good job on me, I would not even consider going back to Moose Jaw to spend a weekend with my grandparents. Oh well, live and learn. That was just one of my questionable unpleasant experiences at Manning Depot.

From Brandon we reported to #7, Bombing and Gunnery training School in Mossbank Saskatchewan. We went there on guard duty, but I believe it was really a means to get us out of the Manning Depot so that they could get more recruits in. The #7 B &G was a temporary holding unit for trainees from the Depot, as well as a flying training unit. We were now on guard duty at this station. I was there for about two months.

It was here I had my first ever airplane ride, I got a chance to fly in the back seat of a Fairey Battle on a maintenance test flight. The Fairey Battle was a single engine day bomber, retired from front line service in the war zones, and modified into a trainer for Bomb Aimers and Air gunners. From 1939 onward, Britain shipped several hundred of these aircraft to Canada, for use in the B & G training schools. The flight was very exciting, and I will never forget the experience. Sure glad they accepted me for Pilot training.

I remember a very cold day during my tour there. An airman with his parka up and paying no attention to taxiing aircraft walked across the tarmac at an angle. A Fairey Battle taxiing out for a training operation, struck the air- man, and the propeller took off half of his head, Unfortunately, I was the guy they sent out to clean up the aircraft. His brains and other gore were all over the landing lights, and when I saw that, I started vomiting. This was my first up front experience with a human's death. I was certainly impressed, but not favourably. Within a few weeks, I reported to Initial Training School (ITS) in Regina Saskatchewan.

This is where we did a lot of bookwork; history, geography, mathematics, aero dynamics, and we must not forget K.R. (Air) (Kings Rules and Regulations). Simply speaking, that was the book of rules and regulations governing the British Commonwealth armed forces, with only minor variations per Country and branch of the services.

The new recruits were assigned to different barrack blocks and each had a name. My billet was the Barker, so named for the Canadian World War 1 Ace, Billy Barker and by coincidence the last name of my grandparents. Sorry, no connection.

It was lights out at 7:00PM. We had permission to go out, to go to town on the weekends but we had to be back in barracks by 9:00PM. We would go to town for a show or a dance, however at this stage in my life I would not dance because of my shyness around women. This I assured myself must change. Sometimes, we would come back to barracks slightly after 9:00PM. On those occasions, we had to outwit the Guard patrols or else.

There was a group of us that discovered a hole under the fence that had been manmade, you understand by whom of course. Our favourite method during my time was to hide behind bushes next to the fence. The first group, returning was responsible for excavating a sizable hole under the fence. In doing so, the excavated earth had to be, pulled back to the outside of the fence. The last group through had the most difficult chore of all, as they must pull the earth back into the excavation. In any event, I have made the whole exercise seem much more simplistic than it was in reality, but believe me it worked, most times.

One night Charlie and I were last to go. He went first because I was much smaller than he was, and, while waiting for the guard to go past I could fill in some of the waste earth. I timed the guard's away time and then crawled under the fence, and as was my duty, filled in the excavation. I then ran to beat hell for my hut, the Barker, which was closest to the fence. I had just reached the door, when the guard shouted HALT! I was in through the door at top speed, and decided I would be better off to go to the far end of the barracks. There would be many people in bed along both sides. The further down the barrack, the safer I would be. I went about half way down and jumped fully clothed into an unoccupied bed, covered myself up with blankets and pretended I was sleeping. Suddenly I remembered I should take my boots off, as I knew he would be looking for them if he got this far. Before I could do so, the guard came through the door and rapidly walked down the row between the beds. Before he got to the bed I had jumped into, he caught two other fellows. The guard was happy with this result but I really caught hell afterwards from the other guys, because I was obviously the one, that brought the guard into the barracks in the first place, and the relative innocents were the ones that were caught.

In May 1942, we went from Initial Training School to #19 EFTS (Elementary Flying Training School) at Virden Manitoba to start our flight training. The first man of authority we met was Flight Lieutenant W. J. McFee, the Chief Flying Instructor. He soon became God in our eyes because he obviously played a big part, in the final decision on whether or not you graduated.

This would really be my first flying, as I previously had only the one flight in the Fairey Battle at Mossbank.

When we arrived at the Virden base, and looked out at the tarmac, there were all these bright yellow bi-planes sitting there, waiting, just for us. They were the De Havilland Tiger Moths. This two- seat biplane was the primary trainer throughout the Commonwealth, well liked by the instructors who flew it, as the flight controls required a positive hand or foot movement to counter the slowness of the aircraft to respond. This apparently assisted the instructors in weeding out uncoordinated student pilots.

The first part of our training was ground school. Here we learned everything pertinent to flying in the local area such as map reading, basic navigation, some meteorology, no-flying areas, and emergency procedures. We learned the functions of the various flight instruments, navigation aids, and mathematics among other things. Around the third or fourth week, we had a half-day of classes, which included time on the link trainer and a half-day of flying.

The Link Trainer was a crude forerunner of today's flight simulator, and used for training on instrument flying. You sat in a cockpit with panel of flight instruments, a stick and rudders and a hood, which lowered to simulate instrument flying conditions. The instructor would sit outside at a desk equipped with the twins of your instruments, and he could see everything you were doing. Although most of us hated it, there is no doubt it served a very useful purpose, in simulating instrument flying conditions.

I will never forget my first real flight. I was a little bit concerned when they started teaching bailing out procedures, however soon realized that this was a very essential part of flying training. If you had an emergency requiring you to abandon your aircraft, you had better do so quickly and correctly the first time because seldom if ever, did you get a second chance.

I flew solo after approximately nine hours of training, which is not much. I sure remember the day, when after a practice landing, and just prior to another take-off, my instructor told me pull over to one side, and I was to go solo for one landing. This was the day we all looked forward to, but when he got out of the aircraft complete with his parachute I all of a sudden felt great trepidation, realizing, it's all up to me. There would be no instructor to give me advice, or more importantly, take control of the aircraft in the event of an emergency. I was on my own now.

Well, let us get on with it. I did all my pre-take off checks and turned the bird into the wind. When the tower gave me the green light, I increased my power for take-off, simultaneously released my brakes, and very quickly, I was airborne. My landing was not great but it was safe. I taxied back and picked up my instructor, and we returned to the hangar. When I got down on terra firma, my instructor shook my hand, and said I had done very well. As we entered the dispatcher's room everybody was clapping and shouting hurrahs. My chest was twice its normal size. What a great day. Now I was the greatest ace in the world, at least in my mind.

I met a girl in Virden, a cute little lass, whom I fell for and we soon became good friends. On my second solo flight, I flew out to her parent's farm. I had made this little parachute out of a handkerchief by tying strings to four corners, bring it down to a point and tying a rock weight on the end. I wrote a little note saying I will meet you in town tonight at 5:30 or 6:00 and we will go to a show or something and I taped it to the parachute. Well I came down low, over the farm, and being the ace that I was, buzzed the farmhouse and they all came running out. Her mom, dad brother and she, all waved at me and I dropped the parachute. Then I thought I would show them my skills.

I staggered the airplane up to about six thousand feet, put it in a dive, and then pulled up doing a loop. Well it was so successful I thought I should do a second one. It was not quite as successful but I staggered over at the top and then, stupid me, I had to try to do a third. Well I just about bought the whole farm at that stage. The plane came up vertical, stalled, the prop stopped and I went into a tailskid and came down backwards. I started panicking; trying to remember all the procedures, I was supposed to do. I kicked her over, went into a dive, and pulled sharply back on the control column (stick) and then, by the grace of God she started. It was not exactly what they told us to do, but whatever I did, it worked. I went straight back to base with underwear that was white when I started, but I am sure there were yellow stains when I got back to base. How stupid can you get? Later on, after we graduated, we heard many other stories, and believe me, I was not the only stupid would be pilot.

When I met her in town that evening and she was telling me how thrilled her parents were by the tremendous show I had put on, I told her "that was nothing you know." Cocky? Yes. Stupid? Yes, but in my defence, I sure learned a great lesson.

Other stories, such as flying under a bridge, were equally as stupid, but there were usually thirty or so aircraft in the air at one time so the powers to be had difficulty figuring out who it was. Lucky for me! If the instructors caught any of us in any of these escapades, it could mean "washing out," which meant you were often discharged, sent home and no longer a pilot in training.

Despite these episodes, it was serious business to get through Elementary Flying Training School. Around the end of June, we completed our training and graduated. What a happy day for us.

On July 2, 1942, it was off to #12 Service Flying Training School (SFTS) in Brandon Manitoba, which is only a stones throw away from Virden. I reported to E Flight of No. 2 Squadron under the command of F/O W.S. Johnson. No.2 Squadron was under the command of K.A.S. Laing. Later on command of No. 2 Squadron became the responsibility of F/L C. H. Mussels, who after the war was my Commanding Officer at 426 Squadron, where I flew the North Star, a four-engine transport. At Brandon, we would train on the Cessna Crane twin-engine aircraft. This is big time now, as this aircraft also had retractable undercarriage.

One of the things that stand out in my memory at this stage in my training was whenever there was a serious accident and a fatality the training officers would take us out and make sure we saw the blood and gore, attributed to, in most cases bad airmanship or carelessness. We did not necessarily know the casualties by name, but we knew they were from our training school and they were dead. This brought home the importance of the professional training we were receiving.

The training was extremely tough here. Classroom training was always a boor to most of us, but it was something, of course very necessary. When we started our night flying, it was initially quite frightening, as we had no experience what so ever in this new environment. However, once we had a few flights under our belts it became very enjoyable.

We also went to ground school and this was heavy duty now. We really got into air navigation in this phase, map reading in day light and basic astronomy at night and of course radio bearings. Today you would probably have thirty hours of training before soloing but then, I think we had around ten or twelve hours. We were not really, what you would call experts but the training in general was fantastic, and the instructors charged with delivering it were superb.

It was now October 1942 and the big day had arrived, Wings Parade! This was the greatest day in our young lives! We lined up on the parade square, under the command of Flight Lieutenant C. H. Mussels. I cannot remember the name of the senior officer, who actually congratulated each of us while fastening our Pilot Wings to our temporarily expanded chests. What a wonderful experience that was. This also was the day, we would find out what our rank was going to be. I graduated as a Sergeant Pilot and the chevrons were quickly sewn onto our jackets. A relative few received their Commissions' to Officer's rank as Pilot Officers.

At this stage, my flying hours totalled 289.30 flying hours, 136.45 as a solo pilot. The assessment of my abilities ***as a T.E. Pilot were Average and as a Pilot-Navigator Average. Points in Airmanship to be watched - Airmanship needs improving.***

Just an average pilot, but I got my wings.

It was also on graduation day we found out what our future assignment would be, when we were to report and where. Forty - six young men out of sixty who commenced SFTS, graduated that day. Thirty- seven, received postings overseas, and nine received assignment to instructor duties in Canada. Of the thirty- seven members of our course who went-overseas, only twelve came home.

CHAPTER THREE
SHIPPING OUT

On October 20, 1942, I wrote to Mr. And Mrs. Matthews, our neighbours in Tuberose, enclosing a short note to my Dad to advise that thirty-seven of the forty-six graduates would be going overseas and I thought I would be one of them. I told him I thought it would be easier for him to break the news to mother than my doing it by letter. I also asked the Matthews family to help break the news to my mother, and to do their best to convince her I would be all right. What a stupid request that was, but who-ever said teenagers were over endowed with the smarts. Just before mailing the letter, I received my orders and so added a postscript saying, ***"Dad, I just found out I'm definitely going over. I have to report on November 7 at Halifax. "***

Some of the boys in the group were, Peter Cumberbirch, Charlie James, (Charlie's mother and my mother were very good friends in Moose Jaw, and now Charlie and I were on the same course) Ivan Moreside, who passed away in 2007, and Ken Petch who is hurting badly with crippling arthritis. These are the ones alive now in 2008. Only four of us left.

We went home on embarkation leave. Now it really hit us, we are really going to war. I came home and spent about a week with my parents and then, another five or six days with grandma and grandpa in Moose Jaw.

I lived with my Grandpa and Grandma for one school year while attending Central Collegiate in Moose Jaw. Grandpa, a

Canadian Pacific Railroad engineer had one time taken me in the locomotive on a trip down to the U.S. border. I remember how he taught me the proper use of the train whistle. When coming into a town it was one long whistle, when passing the town name sign. The level rail crossings were two longs a short and a long, all done with a rope pulley. He let me control the whistle the whole trip. Grandpa also tried to teach me how to pee from a moving train engine. You had to pull back the curtain on the side of the locomotive, as it had no door. You then hang on for dear life and pee, hopefully down wind. I could never do it because of the tremendous rocking back and forth and as a result when we finally reached a stop, my bladder would be ready to explode.

I spent these last few days with them and I recall there was a lot of crying by my Aunt Louise and Grandma. My Grandpa was a real character. His last advice for me was "Keep it in your pants son."

I never really thought about the dramatics involved in leaving those you loved, not just for a day, a week, a month, a year, but maybe forever. Now, as the train started moving, it suddenly hit me, I was shipping out. I remember seeing Grandpa, Grandma, and Aunt Louise through the coach window, standing on the platform waving and crying. That was the first time I had a feeling, a feeling of wondering, would I ever see them again? You must remember this is a farm boy going into a completely new environment, totally, foreign to him.

Some of my cohorts from training were on the same train having boarded at different stops, like Charlie James, who got on at Strasburg, Ivan Moreside, and Ken Petch boarded along the way as well. "The die had been cast." We were now on the first leg of our journey into battle.

The next time we got off the train for an extended period was in Montreal. I cannot really remember but I believe we had two or three days there. I remember we went down to the Red Light district. We walked along the frontage street noting, with a slight amount of embarrassment, the ladies of the night sitting on their balconies in their housecoats, and on many occasions a lot less, waving at us and asking to us to come in. Most of us were very shy country boys, but Charlie gave us the impression that he was much more experienced with this sort of thing. We still kid him about it to this day, as the city slicker who knew all about these things unlike us country boys. I honestly assure you we did not go into any of these places, but I must admit we did walk the full two or three blocks of the houses of ill repute.

We departed from Montreal and went to New York where we had a 48-hour escorted leave. Our departure point had changed from Halifax to New York, as the HMS Queen Elizabeth became available. Little did we realize what a break that was.

We received tickets to a radio talk show and on this particular trip, Gerry Edwards, came with us. (*Post war Wing Commander Gerry Edwards was my Senior Air Staff Officer (SASO) at Air Transport Command Headquarters*)

I will always remember the comedy of the host selecting Gerry from the audience and escorting him up on stage. It was one of these games where the person on stage would say, "In this contest, we have for you, some wonderful prizes, including cash prizes. However, you have to answer all the questions correctly. Now are you ready Pilot Officer Edwards? Yes, I am ready. Are you sure, Pilot Office Edwards? Are you sure, you can answer these questions? You are not nervous or anything? Remember that you only have one chance." Gerry said; "I am ready." "Okay, here is the question. Now remember you only have thirty seconds to answer and all those prizes are yours if you can answer correctly. Have we emphasized that enough?" Gerry said, "Yes, now what is the question?" "The question is; Give us the name of four kinds of nuts." Gerry said "okay, peanuts." The host said; "right, now you only have twenty seconds left; "Walnuts?" "That is right, ten seconds left." "Cashews?" "Right, five seconds left." "Ah, ah, ah DOUGHNUTS!!!" Well everyone in the crowd burst out laughing but poor Gerry got no prizes.

Another first for our group was a visit to the Empire State building. We took the elevator to the top floor where you could see most of the City itself, however as the railing in those days was not enclosed, most of the people would go right up to the iron railing which was about four feet high, and gaze out at the fabulous view. I however, stayed well back, having no desire to enjoy being that close to oblivion. The fellows kept insisting I should come up to the railing, and although I finally did advance, I must admit I grabbed the railing with both hands. I am sure my handprints were actually, deeply implanted in the top rail.

On November 22, 1942, we sailed from New York Harbour. We boarded the Queen Elizabeth and to a man, we were, absolutely amazed at her fantastic size. What a ship! Remember, the only boat any of us had ever been on was a rowboat, not even a motorboat, but a rowboat. Here was this huge ship waiting for us. The Queen Elizabeth was a luxury liner converted to a troop carrier, capable of carrying fifteen thousand troops. During her wartime service, she carried over seven hundred and fifty thousand troops and sailed more than five hundred thousand miles.

The next beautiful site was the magnificent Statue of Liberty seemingly waving good- bye as we left the New York Harbour, and more importantly the North American Continent. There were many misgivings, and many sniffles, yes, also many man -sized tears. Obviously, we eighteen and nineteen year olds were not as brave as we thought we were.

The talk on board ship centered on the fantastic number of troops and their gear she was carrying. Because of the number of men on board, we only got two full meals a day. After we set sail, the daily routine consisted of lining up for breakfast at 5:00 in the morning, and by the time, you got through having your breakfast it might be 9:00 or 10:00. With these great long line-ups, it was not long before it was time to start lining up for dinner. Thank God, we had numerous canteens on every deck, which sufficed for filling the stomach holes, which seemed to make their presence known between the major meals.

We obviously had lots of spare time on our hands to explore her majesty, and I remember going to the front of the ship. Oh how I loved it up there! We hit some very rough seas and I remember the prow of the ship going up in the air, and then crashing down into the ocean. A number of the men were honking their guts up, but I loved it. I never felt a bit sick.

Meanwhile back inside it was time to start lining up for dinner. The standard procedure for food servers was to fill up your plate with potatoes, fried chicken, gravy and veggies and a great desert on a separate dish. The meals were always first class, and there was seldom if ever, repetition of the main courses.

As general practice when I left the serving line-up, I would scan the dining room looking for a sickly looking fellow, and then sit as close as I could to my potential victim, preferably right across the table from him. My next move was to commence talking about things like greasy food or "did you ever find a hair, a human hair in your soup" and this kind of thing. The fellow is fighting the nausea, but then all of a sudden he cannot handle it anymore and he's up and gone. You might feel sorry for the poor fellow, but I would counter that with, obviously he was not going to enjoy his meal even IF and I emphasize IF he could keep it down, where as I had a second meal, and no food was wasted. We did not get seconds because who was going to stand in that long line-up again.

We had another exciting moment on this passage across the ocean when we were all in having dinner. The Queen Elizabeth did not have any escorts. There were no destroyers or frigates. The so-called experts looked at the "no escort" philosophy from the point of view that the QE was a very fast ship, and her speed alone would allow her to outrun a suspected U- boat. This fact soon outweighed the alternative of having a huge target travelling in a convoy, at a speed set by the slowest ship in the convoy, which may be as slow as twenty percent of the Queens normal cruising speed, Obviously there was no argument as to which tactic was the safest.

On the third day at sea, we heard gunfire seemingly from our ship. This ship only had a couple of guns and they were up front. I think they were more of a decorative feature than anything else. The ship made a hard turn to starboard and then a hard turn back to port. Dishes were skidding off the tables, which had an approximate half- inch lip on their edges to keep the dishes from sliding off. All we heard were the guns firing, and the bedlam associated with breaking dishes etc. There were those amongst us who believed a torpedo had hit us and we were likely sinking. There was no doubt some thought we were going to the bottom of Davy Jones' Locker because some damn sub got us. I do not feel we should criticize those frightened believers; after all, at least the vast majority of those on board the "Lizzie" were professional "Land Lubbers." Sometime later, someone advised over the public address system, the lookouts sighted a sub and took rather violent evasive action as a standard defensive measure. That was the last and only real exciting event on the crossing. On November 30, 1942, we disembarked at Prestwick, in Scotland.

CHAPTER FOUR
ARRIVAL IN BOURNEMOUTH

We were now in the United Kingdom, but we did not have much time to celebrate, as it was straight off the ship and onto trains. We were loaded onto several of these British trains and headed down south to Bournemouth.

Bournemouth was one of the most beautiful spots in England, a tourist's paradise. The town itself and most if not all of its lovely tourist hotels had been completely taken over by the military (mostly Canadian Air Force). The beautiful beaches had all these tank traps on them. It was almost disgraceful to see these magnificent natural beaches marred by all these manmade tank traps, however after a few days of living here, and hearing the wail of the air raid siren almost daily, they gave you a small feeling of security.

We had a spell of approximately four weeks there, with nothing to do but eat, sleep and pub-crawl. One afternoon there was an attack by several enemy fighter planes. They strafed (steady machine gun/cannon fire) the beach, and I remember rushing up to the top of our apartment hotel, which was three stories, and onto the roof deck to see all the fireworks. Stupid you know, but I had to make sure I did not miss anything.

We went to dances at the Trianon ballroom in Boscombe on our days off. At one of these dances, I met a very attractive little Irish nurse. I noticed her standing back and not dancing, and I realized I was doing the same thing, just watching people dance. I was not much of a dancer, maybe a waltz or a fox trot were about the only dances in my repertoire, and even with these I certainly was no match for even a one legged Fred Astaire. Well I finally got up enough nerve, went over to her, and started talking. We hit it off real quick so we started to dance and only danced with one another all night. When it came time to go back to the barracks, I asked her if it would be all right if I took her home. She replied; "that would be very nice." So away we went, walking of course.

We went around one corner and there were about eight or ten soldiers of the Scottish Black Watch Regiment huddled there. They almost immediately started saying things that I had never heard anyone say in front of women before. This made me very angry, because in my humble book this kind of talk was absolutely, wrong. I turned to go back, and she grabbed my arm and said "Don't go back; they will kill you!" I replied, "They can't talk to you that way!" They were saying things like "You going to fuck her tonight Canada". Well I had never in my life heard that word used in the presence of a woman. In fact, I had never even heard that word, until I joined the service. Anyway, I headed back to the guilty parties. That was another stupid Canadian farm boy trick.

When I started lecturing them on their lack of respect for a lady, they started to laugh and one came at me. I could handle myself pretty well, but the odds were too lopsided, too much on their side. I had no chance in the world, and although I got a couple of good punches in, they beat the hell out of me. I ended up with another Canadian airman, hauling me back to the barracks on his back. I had a broken rib and they had stolen my money belt with about sixty pounds in it, which was a hell of a lot of money in those days, about three hundred dollars to be precise. That was almost my total savings for the last three or four months. We were only making peanuts $3.70 per day or something like that. Anyway, that was another lesson, diplomacy first until you fully evaluate the situation. You do not fight unless the odds are at least even.

I was very concerned about the fate of my little Irish nurse; however, the airman, who took me back to our digs, said he had hailed a cab and paid the cabby to take her home. I promised to repay him when we got back to our barracks

We had many fights. The Black Watch did not like us because they thought we had all kinds of extra luxuries that they did not. They call us the "Brylcream Boys."

I remember another time going into a pub, and it seemed it was always the same routine. There would be Black Watch and RCAF/RAF in the pub. The Black Watch would be standing or sitting on one side and the RCAF/RAF on the other side. We would all be drinking beer, big pints. Then all of a sudden, it would be like magic. Back would go the chairs. Well I sized things up pretty well beforehand and saw this little fellow. He was mine! The chairs went back and I rushed over to him. We were nicely throwing punches at each other and all of a sudden, I saw stars! I came to under a table. I had been cold cocked on top of the head with a bottle by somebody behind me! However, there was a hell of a good fight going on and I realized I was missing it. I came out from under the table and was about to get into it when WHAM! I saw stars again! Somebody had seen my head coming out from under the table and hit me again! The next thing I knew, one of my mates carried me home. This was another good lesson! Be very careful who is behind you when you are fighting.

In Bournemouth, we had a lot of physical training. Our PTI (physical training instructor) was the runner up in the light heavy weight boxing championship in Britain. He took a group of about five or six of us little fellows and put a lot of emphasis on boxing. He said, "You boys are automatically going to get into lots of fights because we have bullies, lots of bullies, and bullies always pick on the little chaps." He taught us all the tricks of how to fight dirty. I remember him telling us if we had a big chap standing next to us in a bar and he starts to stir something up, be nice to him, smile, and go along with whatever he says. Then the first chance you get when you have him believing you are a nice enough fellow, you grab him behind the head, pull it forward and then bring your knee up into his crotch and your head right into his face as hard as you can. If that does not drop him, start running because that is the only alternative you have. Anyway, his training worked quite well.

Well that was Bournemouth.

CHAPTER FIVE
FLIGHT TRAINING IN BRITAIN

After our adjustment time in Bournemouth, the army took some of us for high-intensity training. I trained with the Royal Canadian Regiment from Ottawa. I was with them for three weeks during which time we did everything on the double. We were not allowed to walk anywhere on the base. We ran!! We went on marches of twelve to fifteen miles, jogging with full packs on our backs and carrying rifles. We would go through a range with low barbed wire, about eighteen inches off the ground, with lots of animal entrails under the wire and machine gun fire going over top so you would keep your head down. We had to crawl through this, through all these entrails. Many got sick in there, believe me.

Well I got through that and I reported to #26 EFTS (Elementary Flying Training School) at Theale, Berkshire training on the De Havilland 82 Tiger Moths again. I was there from February 19 until March 19, 1943. There was nothing very special about Theale that I remember other than I got about forty more hours of flying in and studied map reading British style, just to show us what it was like flying in their country. This was no doubt to pacify our boredom and anxiousness at the slow process of getting into action.

My summary of flying and assessments read *"as a pilot - above average, as a pilot/navigator - good average, Points in Flying or Airmanship which Should be Watched - Nil"* Better rating than my last one.

From there I reported to the Advanced Flying Unit (#14 AFU) in Ossington, Nottinghamshire where I trained on twin engine Oxfords from April 1 to May 9, 1943. In addition, I spent about a week at #1518 Beam Approach Training at Scampton Lincolnshire.

Beam Approach was an automatic radar landing system. It transmitted dots on one side of the runway and dashes for the other side allowing the pilot to determine the aircrafts position relative to the runway. *"Assessment average".*

When I got through that, I reported in June to #81 OTU in Tilstock Shropshire, an operational training unit for the Whitley. Oh boy! Finally! They were those funny looking twin-engine bombers that flew in a nose down attitude. They only had a speed of around one hundred knots, but they were big and very heavy, and at last, we were flying a real bomber.

It was here, in Tilstock I again took a girl up in the aircraft and I should not have. I believe she was in an organization known as Land Watch. They wore green shirts and trousers and did a lot of work helping the farmers in the agricultural fields.

She was quite attractive. I was still quite shy with women, but I took her up in the Whitley for about an hour and a half. I discovered later what the fellows meant when they asked if I had joined the mile high club. I still thought it was awful that they talked this way. I was once again lucky the instructor's did not catch me, as it would have meant washing out or in other words, sent home. This is what they told us, however, no one had ever heard of a pilot sent home.

We went through the initial training, checkouts and then we were sent to a large room with navigators, gunners, bomb aimers, wireless operators, and flight engineers for the sole purpose of selecting a crew. There might be ten or twelve pilots in the room. I found this very interesting. I did not know what I was looking for, nor did most of the crewmembers present. It was up to the pilot to get the ball rolling.

Those who were there for the first time, as well as experienced crews, generally accepted during the crew selection process, in order to enhance their chances of survival, it was imperative a bomber crew must be more closely knit than they were with their own family. Simply said, each crewmember must independently execute his specific duties in an above average manner if the crew's chances of defeating the "Grim Reaper" were to become a reality. Needless- to- say, as the experience level associated with successful operations increases, so does the possibility of over confidence raising its ugly head. This is why the pilot, who is always the designated captain, regardless of rank, is responsible for ensuring, to the best of his ability, that non-conformance is not acceptable, and guilty crewmembers, must be replaced if the situation did develop. Fortunately, our crew was extremely well knit and said situation never occurred.

With respect to the crew selection process, we, the pilots, were obviously novices at this and therefore one would suspect the whole process was likely amateurish. For myself, I made a point of talking to as many people as possible on the first day.

As I recall, sixty- seven years ago, my first pick in the last hour or so of day one, was Kenneth (Archie) Archibald, rear gunner. Archie was a little Scotsman, who impressed me with his Scottish brogue, his sense of humour, and his desire to get at the enemy as soon as possible. On the second day, F/O Don Holder, a Canadian navigator from Brandon, Manitoba approached me. After about thirty minutes of idle chitchat, I asked him to join the crew, to which he agreed. Shortly thereafter, I noticed Bernard (Bernie) Pullin, a Bomb Aimer standing off by himself. It was quite apparent he was not getting much attention, so Archie, Don, and I went over and introduced ourselves. Bernie appeared to be overly shy, but was obviously very pleased we had come over to him. After a few minutes of general conversation, I came away with the feeling he would be well worth having as a crewmember despite his obvious shyness. We excused ourselves and moved a few paces away from him, at which time he appeared to be very sad. I asked the other two what they thought of having him as a member of our crew. They shared my feelings, so we walked back to him and I asked him if he would like to join our crew. He immediately replied, "I would be honoured to do so."

We appeared to be making great progress with our recruiting process, simplistic, as this was, however we still had to find a Wireless Operator/Air Gunner, a Mid Upper Gunner, and a Flight Engineer.

We then met John "Corny" Broad. The nickname Corny was obviously, because he was from Cornwall. Much like Archie, he seemed to have a good sense of humour with one of his first admissions being "yes I do like broads, and yes, I normally pick good ones." Due to my ignorance on the subject, I was not able to establish where he was coming from; however, the rest of our new crew, with the possible exception of Bernie, laughed loudly at Corny's admission. We now had our Wireless Operator/Air Gunner and had only to find a Flight Engineer and Mid Upper Gunner.

I explained to my new crew, that a good Engineer was extremely important. Once we were over enemy territory, if engine problems occurred, the Engineer, because of his training, might be able to correct the problem. If not, then his assessment of its seriousness would be invaluable to me in reaching a decision on whether or not to abort the operation. I then suggested to the present crew they should look for another Gunner or two who they would consider strong candidates. I would take on the responsibility of looking for a good candidate for Flight Engineer.

My other motive for personally selecting a Flight Engineer was a direct result of a very unusual situation present within the Lancaster itself. All other medium and heavy bombers in the R.A.F., the U.S.A.F. and Commonwealth Air forces, were usually crewed with two pilots. The Lancaster did not have dual controls or even a seat for a co-pilot. It was suggested by our Pilot Instructors, we, the aircraft Captains, give whatever training we could to our Engineers while on navigational or other friendly territory flying exercises, so in the event the Captain was seriously wounded or killed, the Engineer could at least fly the aircraft back to friendly territory where the crew could bail out.

I walked amongst the dozens of aircrew, looking for a man wearing an Engineers badge. When I discovered one, I would strike up a conversation centered on did he have any flying experience? Would he like to be a pilot? I finally ended up with a rather tall, athletically built young man from

Lancashire named John Rawcliffe. John gave me more or less the same kind of questionnaire I had given him. I was very impressed with John and when I asked him if he would like to join our crew, he said he would like to meet them before making a decision. I took John over to the others who by this time had found a Mid Upper Gunner candidate by the name of Chris Poulton. After more conversation, both agreed to join up with us, and to say I was happy with the picks would be an understatement of the first order. We now wanted to get our training completed so we could commence our tour of operations. I believe this responsibility took me from being a boy to a man.

I have seen many different views on the subject of rank differential amongst crews during the war. I believe there are some basics, which must be entertained.

The personal relationship between different ranks varied from crew to crew; however, I believe the way I operated was the norm on RAF Squadrons.

The pilot is the skipper (Captain) from the time the crew boards the aircraft, thus rank structure once on board is non-existent. I was a Flight Sergeant and my navigator was a Flying Officer. Once airborne and when and if conversation was absolutely necessary, members of the crew, talked as briefly as possible from station to station with the Captain's permission, and only on matters pertinent to the operation at hand.

The Royal Air Force did not permit members to be out of uniform when off the station. Our crew was always in uniform, even on leave. As to how I related to my crew, I honestly liked them after we finished our operational training and by the time we had completed our first fifteen or twenty operations, they had become my family, and to this day, I truly loved them like brothers.

It was here at Tilstock, I experienced what is referred to as incidents, which were not entered in my logbook. On the 15 of June 1943 while flying as a "pupil pilot," with F/O L. Hewitt as the pilot and F/Sgt. C.Gracie as the Instructor, the following took place. *"After being airborne for 1 hr and 50 minutes, the Engine RPM Indicator showed a drop in the port engine revs. The screened pilot (Hewitt) raised the pitch lever to regain normal cruising revs, but without success. In two minutes time nothing at all registered on the port RPM indicator. The aircraft swung to port and emergency procedure carried out, a successful forced landing resulted at Weston Leyland. In the report known as "Report on Flying Accident or Forced Landing Not Attributable to Enemy Action (Form 766 ©) the remarks of the S/L. Robertson, the unit commander were as follows: "A drop in the revs. On the port engine occurred after 1 hour and 50min. of flying time. This loss could not be regained by manipulation of pitch control lever and eventually the rev. counter showed nothing. There was an apparent loss of power so a single engine landing was carried out at the nearest aerodrome. The failure of the red light indicator was due to mechanical failure of the engine speed indicator, resulting in indicated loss of revs. The screened pilot took immediate and correct action and got down at the nearest aerodrome without damage to the aircraft or injury to the crew. Log Book Endorsement not recommended."*

The second incident took place on June 22/43. I was the pilot and the instructor was not flying with us that day. *Whilst flying at 6000 ft. on a cross country, the port RPM indicator showed a rise in revs, the exactor control was depressed to synchronize the engine, but the revs continued to rise, so a landing was carried out to investigate the trouble. The aircraft was flown back to base at 1720 hrs the same day. The report from the Unit Commander was as follows: "After approximately one hour and a half flying, the port constant speed unit went u/s resulting in the propeller going to the fully fine position. The pilot throttled back and carried out a landing at the nearest aerodrome. The cause of the propeller going to the fully fine position was due to the fact that the hydraulic feed line to the C.S.4 was fractured resulting in a loss of pressure and the C.S.4. became unserviceable. The pupil pilot took the correct immediate action and landed successfully at the nearest aerodrome. Log Book Endorsement not recommended."*

I completed my training on July 29, 1943, with an additional eighty-six or eighty- seven hours of flying time. The assessment of my ability as a MB Pilot recorded in my logbook ***"above the average" Points in airmanship, which should be watched - Nil.*** In my R.A.F. Training Report, I scored 71% average in my Ground Examinations and 82% in my Flying Tests. In the Assessment of qualities of Character and Leadership, I achieved 88% and the remarks of S/L C.V. Masters were as follows: ***"An above average pilot. Has done well on the course and will most certainly make a very good operational captain. An excellent type, keen and conscientious. Recommended for a commission. Form 1020A completed."*** I received a promotion from Flight Sergeant to Warrant Officer, class 2

Around August 15, 1943, we commenced flying at #1662 Conversion Unit in Blyton, Lincolnshire. This was the training unit for heavy bombers.

We started there on the Halifax, which was a four-engine bomber, and then on to the Lancaster. We trained on the

Halifax August 15 - 21, a total of fifteen hours and the Lancaster from Sept. 14 - October 2, 1943 for about thirty hours.

This became an extremely interesting part of our career because point one: we boarded these huge four engine aircraft and there was only one pilot seat. The aircraft crew for a Lancaster did not include a co-pilot. "How do they train us?" Well the instructor sat in the engineer's seat. We had the controls and he would talk us through takeoff and landings, this of course was after very extensive briefings. "What a thrill! To get in these huge airplanes, you cannot imagine the size of these things. One hundred and three foot wing spans, and they carried thousands of pounds of bombs" Well I graduated as a pilot, with an assessment ***as a HB pilot - above average and no points in airmanship to be watched.***

When I got my wings, I wanted to be a fighter pilot. I thought I had a good chance because I was small in stature and fighter plane cockpits are anything but roomy. However, those who made the decisions posted me as a bomber pilot on the biggest damned planes they had. My cockpit seat was twenty-one feet above the ground I even had to sit on an extra cushion so I could see where I was going. It was quite an experience. I checked out, successfully on the aircraft, and our crew started flying together, doing cross-countries, live gun firing exercises, and practice bombing. In the meantime, we were waiting for our graduation party from the conversion unit and our first posting to an operational unit.

Our pre-operational training should have included a "nickel" raid. A nickel raid involved dropping propaganda pamphlets over cities, towns, and other high-density French targets bordering the English Channel. These sorties also provided new crews with an opportunity to experience searchlights and light to medium flak over enemy territory. The sortie was a final crew training exercise. Our crew never made such a trip, and I do not know why, especially since this exercise was considered standard practice.

The first truly operational flight for new Captains was to go on an operation as an observer with an experienced crew. You would fly with an experienced captain and his crew solely for the purpose, of experiencing the sometimes numerous unforeseen decisions requiring the Captain's on the spot immediate action. I never got this so-called experience trip, and again I do not know why! I do not in fact know to this day why.

CHAPTER SIX

101 SQUADRON
LUDFORD MAGNA

"Mens agitat molem" (Mind over Matter)

On October 11, 1943, we reported to 101 Squadron at Ludford Magna, Lincolnshire, which was a special duties Squadron. We did not know what that meant at the time.

Ludford Magna was a new station and garnered the nickname "Mudford Magna" almost immediately. There was mud everywhere, all over the roads and taxiways, everywhere.

Shortly thereafter, senior officers briefed us on what our special duties consisted of, which was very interesting. We now carried an eighth crewmember that was not necessarily with us regularly. We had an extra, massive bank of radios carried in the crew compartment, covering literally hundreds of frequencies. The special radio operators job on a raid, was to search the whole spectrum of frequencies, and pick up those being used by the Luftwaffe radar control units, who were vectoring their fighters on to the bomber stream, and if necessary on to specific targets. He spoke fluent German and could effectively jam the Luftwaffe controllers by squelching their frequencies; the exercise was usually successful although limited to some degree by the vast number of frequencies they had to monitor.

The aircraft carrying these extra radio experts had specific take off times, which to some degree, controlled their spacing throughout the bomber stream thus avoiding over-lapping. It worked well but we suffered tremendous losses of crews and aircraft as the Luftwaffe night- fighter aircrews started homing in on our jamming frequencies. If their Messerschmitt 110s or Junker 88s remained undetected by our aircrews, the odds were definitely against us, and the enemy fighters would be credited with yet another victory.

It was about this time that our Intelligence was getting reports that the Luftwaffe were modifying the Junker's 88 armament system, to enable them to attack with cannons and/ or machine guns aligned at approximately forty-five degrees from well below the target, that definitely would be in our blind zone, and would give them a great advantage. Too bad, they took the belly turret out of the Lancaster way back when. The supposed modification of the Ju88 was interesting, but if it becomes factual, our losses would definitely increase. God forbid.

This armament modification came to be and the JU88 was equipped with the Schrage Musik cannon armament, a twin twenty millimetre cannon mounted in the fuselage of the Junkers, immediately behind the cockpit, which fired at a forty-five degree angle. This became the standard upward firing armament of the German night-fighters in 1944 and 1945 and we would later experience the disastrous results of an attack by this method.

On November 3, 1943, I checked the Battle Order posting. We were not included. Chris, our mid upper gunner, was assigned to F/S J.M.Cummings crew that night, for an operation to Dusseldorf. Their aircraft did not return and I can only assume Chris was killed in action, as I was never able to find out any other information about him.

We now had the task of replacing him. We picked up Sgt. A. Kirton, who flew with us for the rest of our time with 101 Squadron and sustained injuries on our last sortie from Ludford Magna.

We went on leave from November 9 to November 15, but never left the local area. Following expiration of our leave we were on the Battle Order of our new Squadron, the date was November 18/43. Now the sweating started. History records this date as the commencement of the Battle of Berlin.

All the crews listed on the Battle Order filed into this large operational briefing room, Service Police stationed at the entry doors, ensured only valid personnel entered. A large wall covered entirely with curtains was at the front of the room along with a podium for officers charged with briefing us. We saw all these curtains draped over the wall behind the podium, and realized they were covering information that would soon be brought to our attention, but absolutely nothing in the room indicates the target for tonight's raid. The Station CO entered the room and all present came to attention on the Squadron Commander's orders. The CO then takes his seat. Our Squadron Commander starts the briefing with "Gentlemen, this is operation number 1205, and our target for tonight is;" at which time one of the Sergeants in attendance opens one of the drapes displaying a very large map. Our Squadron Commander simultaneously says "the Capital of Germany, Berlin." The reaction in the room is one of "ohs" and groans followed by silence, and he continues; "I am now going to turn you over to our Squadron Operations Officer who will give you an initial briefing on the target."

We are all sitting there with our hearts pounding and they roll down the rest of the curtains. Well the map is very large and very detailed. We are looking at it trying to figure out just where our target is located, when suddenly it hits us again, BERLIN! OUR FIRST TRIP!!!

This was rather disconcerting, as a Berlin target was one of the furthest, distance wise into Germany and as expected, being the German capital, would be very well defended by their fighters and heavy flak installations.

The Operations Officer points out target tracks to and from the target. We are advised what the expected weather will be during the operation. The intelligence officer gets up and shows us the location of all the main ack ack batteries, where all the Luftwaffe fighter bases were located en route, the type of fighter aircraft that would be trying to locate us, and finally where our target aiming point was located.

There were to be four hundred and forty Lancasters and four mosquitoes taking part in the operation. There was also to be two diversionary raids on Mannheim and Ludwigshafen involving three hundred and ninety five aircraft. We learned later that the diversion forces met with heavy German fighter activity and twenty- three aircraft were lost.

The specialist briefings continued for the best part of an hour, at the conclusion of which we pick up our parachutes, mae wests and other operational gear. In the parachute section, they have a big sign that says, "We are very proud of our workmanship when we are repacking your chutes, how-ever if you have to use yours and it doesn't work, bring it back and we will give you another one." Subtle humour I believe. I cannot recall ever hearing of any one being upset by the sign.

It is interesting to note that the Geneva Convention states that we cannot deliberately bomb a city. We can only bomb military targets. However, in the target vocabulary produced by the Geneva Convention, a Post Office is considered a military target. So on many occasions, what we had as an aiming point was a post office.

Trucks then took us out to our aircraft dispersal area. John and I have concluded our external inspection, and all crewmembers have stowed their flight gear in the aircraft, and have satisfied themselves that their station's operational equipment is functioning satisfactorily. Now is the time we would normally end up with idle chit- chat with our ground crew, however tonight was not what one would call normal. In fact, this was somewhat of a real scary time. Here we are, this new crew with no experience of anybody shooting at us, not even knowing what it is like to have a near miss flak burst, about to take off on a raid to one of the most heavily defended areas, and deepest penetrations into enemy territory, BERLIN. I would suggest any one of even average intelligence, who could say they were not at all concerned, would not be telling the truth.

One of the questions most often asked by the generations too young to have served in WWII is "Were you ever scared when you were flying operations over enemy territory?" My answer is always the same. "Any member of the armed services involved in actual combat with the enemy who says they were never scared, falls into one of two categories. They either have the "Gold Medal" for the "Liars Club of the World" or they are prime candidates for a Mental Institution."

In my case, the worst time for potential misgivings occurred when we had finished our external checks on our aircraft, and had completed a very essential tête a tête with our ground crew.

At this time, we were quietly sitting around awaiting the signal from the Control Tower to fire up our engines. All signals up to and including take off are by coloured lamp from the tower, absolutely no instructions are given orally. This procedure was to prevent interception by unfriendly sources, of take-off times and number of aircraft involved in an obvious raid. Once I was in the cockpit and had completed confirmation from each crewmember that their station's equipment was serviceable, I was all business.

To the best of my knowledge throughout all of our trips, my crew never discussed the heavy losses sustained by Bomber Command in general and the Pathfinder forces in particular, nor did we ever discuss the odds of our completing a double tour of forty- five operations as Pathfinders, which was less than four percent. It was not a case of us trying to ignore a "fact of life" but rather if we concentrated on doing the best job possible, we could be part of the three to four percent. Our ground crew strived as well for this goal. I know from discussions with the Sergeant in charge of our ground crew they had a very close relationship with us, and never felt entirely at ease about their workmanship until the aircraft returned home with their precious crew intact. We all appreciated their apparent idolatry very much and we knew when we returned, and the engines shut down, the ground crew would be there to greet each crewmember as they left the aircraft, with loud cheers and a clap on the back.

All of a sudden, we are on our first operational trip, but would you believe going to Berlin, for crying out loud! There we were sitting around the aircraft and everybody was very quiet. There was not a lot of conversation, just thinking. The ground crew was there, doing their checks, assuring us that the aircraft was in beautiful shape. Our ground crew took a very personal interest: this is their aircrew. All of a sudden, a caution light from the tower and it is time to get aboard the aircraft.

Now before we board the rear gunner (Archie) has to go and pee on the tail wheel. Almost all the crews carried out this tradition prior to boarding on every trip, and it is actually a part of Bomber Command history.

We get on board, fire up the engines and complete our pre flight check. Then we get the visual light from the tower to taxi. We get in line with those ahead of us and prepare to take off. Radio silence is imperative.

In our squadron, there were twenty- three aircraft assigned to this target. All of us lined up, engines running, and the green light goes on. The first aircraft goes the second follows and so on. Now it is our turn. Fear is not really an issue; there is a job to do. Away we go, the first takeoff with a full load of bombs, and I think, A FULL LOAD OF BOMBS! Our aircraft was carrying ten thousand five hundred and sixty six pounds of high intensity explosives, so it is a little bit of a different takeoff from the norm. You have to build up a higher speed and make sure you lift off obviously, before reaching the end of the runway. As we become airborne, the first silent sigh of relief comes from all concerned. Now all crewmembers are busy carrying out their duties, as we climb to our designated altitude while merging with other squadrons, prior to reaching the enemy coast. Our altitude was normally a maximum of sixteen to twenty thousand feet.

Perhaps, our gravest concern en route was "in flight collisions." We would spread out here and there and concentrate on staying clear of other aircraft. All gunners, the flight engineer, bomb aimer and captain, had to be very alert all the way to the target and return, while the navigator must do everything possible to arrive on target at our pre-planned time, and en route ensure we avoided all known ack- ack sites. On these raids, we normally ran an average of six hundred to nine hundred aircraft, nearly all of which were four-engine bombers, with a small number of twin engine Mosquitoes in our midst. Once again, I must emphasize that all crews had to be extremely alert because there were bombers all around us, above and below. To provide a picture, imagine looking up and seeing a stream of aircraft that at times could be one mile wide and fifty miles long. The gunners would call out "there's one to your right" or "there's one just above!" and in each case, dependent on location of the other aircraft, he would direct the Captain to take evasive action.

We saw several mid air collisions between our own bombers, albeit, less than one would imagine. In addition, on several occasions we saw Lancasters or Halifaxs catch fire after being attacked by enemy fighter aircraft. If the coloured markers spewing out of the damaged aircraft were the same colour as ours, we knew it was a squadron mate.

We never actually saw crews parachute from these aircraft, but on at least two sorties, we saw burning bombers blow up, and virtually fall in pieces. In both cases, we still had not reached our targets, and their bomb loads were obviously still aboard. This made a fantastic huge ball of fire. When we got over the target, I am sure there were many bombs from the aircraft above that hit our own airplanes. Nevertheless, it was a calculated risk we had to take.

The outbound trip was relatively normal with the usual small alterations to our course to avoid collisions with other friendly aircraft, as well as to circum- navigate areas our intelligence briefing had advised were the home of heavy anti- aircraft batteries. After we crossed the enemy coast, the navigator would call out "there is a defended area coming up on your starboard, about twenty kilometres away." So we would make damn sure we steered clear of that site. This would go on all the way to the target. Archie and Sgt. Kirton kept watch and continued to warn of aircraft close by, or if one went down. They would say, "There is an aircraft to our starboard such and such a distance, don't know what it is at the moment" or they would identify it. Sometimes they would be unable to identify if the aircraft was friendly or not. The Germans even did that well.

There was a certain number of our aircraft that had force landed in enemy territory and unfortunately, the Germans, after making them air worthy, would put them up in the bomber stream. All of a sudden, one of the gunners might see another Lancaster and would call out "stay away from him." It might well be one of our own, but we did not know for sure and neither did they. If you got too close, they friendly or otherwise just might begin firing on you, warning you to get the hell away. This potential hazard would occur all the way to the target and quite often most of the way back.

The target, on major raids, was usually three and a half to four hours away. Sometimes we would go to point A as a diversion and then turn back toward the target. This was to confuse the enemy ground radar as to where our actual target was located. With Pathfinders, which we joined later on, we would fly to a point as if we were going to Dusseldorf and would have all the bombers heading towards Dusseldorf. At a certain point, the Pathfinders would send on a group of planes to Dusseldorf as a spoof. The main bomber stream would then alter their course and attack the main target. All of this of course, was to confuse the enemy fighter planes and their control radar. Although the planned effectiveness was any-ones guess, it no doubt worked to a large degree. In any event, the Spoof Raids when effective at drawing the enemy fighters away from the main force would obviously, result in heavier losses to the Spoof Force.

Getting back to our current operation, we were dropping window, which was shredded tinsel similar to tinfoil. It shows up on the German radar as a target. It also creates an impression on their radar- scopes, of a much greater number of attacking bomber aircraft than there were in reality.

All of a sudden, we see our first enemy flak bursts which dramatically increased in numbers and density, as we got closer to Berlin. Although the flak bursts and tracers, accompanied by sweeping search lights put on a fabulous fourth of July light display, the tremendous explosive sound of near miss flak bursts and the noise of shrapnel striking the fuselage were disconcerting to say the least.

Veteran crews advised the new comers if you could hear the flak explosions you were OK. It was the ones you could not hear that killed you. Very quickly, the explosions brought us back to the reality of our current situation.

The length of time we were in the heavy ack depended on many factors. For example if your target was visual as opposed to cloud covered, you would normally anticipate considerably more ack ack, and the target itself often dictated the number of anti aircraft batteries assigned to its site. Berlin, the capital city was very heavily defended where- as a buzz bomb battery might only have minimal ack ack protection.

Following the bomb release, I started a slow descent with a natural increase in speed and as I cleared the target area, I started a slow turn to the starboard and levelled out when I reached my homeward heading as directed by the Navigator. For the next fifteen to twenty minutes after we released our bombs, I routinely warned both Gunners to be on the alert for enemy fighter aircraft. The whole scenario was eerie to say the least, and I have thought in retrospect fear should have been a factor. However, I was so busy carrying out my essential duties that I can honestly say fear never entered my mind during the course of the battle. I cannot speak for the rest of the crew, as by design, we did not ever discuss the subject.

Our departure from Berlin in particular, and as we discovered later, all major targets in general, depended upon where you were in the bomber stream as to how long you were in the flak. From the time your final attack run commenced, there would be a steady increase in the volume and a variance of height of the ack ack explosions.

Suddenly, all hell would break loose! There were explosions all around us; many of them so close they would rock the aircraft. There were many times we heard the explosions and many times the fuselage would be holed by shrapnel. It did not take long before I learned a little trick.

When I looked up ahead at the flak coming up over the target area, I would say to myself, "there's no way I can get through that, no way", so all I did was lower my seat and fly on instruments. That tactic not only prevented me from seeing all the explosions on our track, but also at the same time gave Bernie a steady platform to operate from in the final few minutes prior to bomb release. Bernie could now see the target marker and started giving me bombing run instructions, "bomb doors open, right steady, steady, left steady, bombs away, bomb bay closed." As soon as the bombs released and Bernie confirmed we had no "hang ups" we would get the hell out of there as quickly as possible. Some pilots would make sharp 180-degree turns, but I adopted a modus operandi of diving straight ahead, thereby quickly increasing speed and decreasing the time in the heaviest flak area. My manoeuvre seemed to work pretty well.

On the return flight, we had to be extremely alert. Now the Germans know where we are, and most of the Luftwaffe fighter aircraft are likely in our stream. We would really have to sweat blood to avoid them. When we flew over the target, the fighters would not normally follow us as their own flak might hit them, but some were a little braver or stupid, and would follow you in. I had that experience, but not on this trip.

We did a corkscrew when we were leaving the target, which means diving to port and then turning to starboard while climbing, turning, and diving again. This was to keep the fighters off your tail. It was extremely important however that you varied your climbing and diving turns, otherwise the enemy fighter could stand off until you gave your routine away, then good-bye Mr. Lancaster. Whenever any member of our crew spotted a fighter, I would immediately go into a corkscrew, by turning in to the fighter. In other words, if the enemy aircraft came from your port side, you would turn left on your first dive or climb manoeuvre. The "cork screw" was the most successful defensive manoeuvre available to the bomber forces. It was extremely effective when executed properly, however it was also very strenuous to execute even for the strongest pilots. Because of its great reputation, there will be numerous times I will speak about it in this story.

We remained alert all the way back to our home base, and I mean all the way back, because there would often be enemy aircraft circling in our own circuit. The Germans would put in sneak aircraft fighters to follow us back and then they would nail us when we were in the circuit or landing pattern while we were most vulnerable.

After we landed and taxied back to our dispersal area, we heaved a great sigh of relief. Archie, the rear gunner, always got out and kissed the pavement. While waiting for our crew transport, we normally had the time to tell our ground crew a little bit about the raid and of course, how the aircraft performed. I would also have to list any engine or airframe problems in the L14 form and sign in. We would then proceed to debriefing, get a coffee, maybe with a little rum in it, and then our intelligence officers would interview crew after crew on what took place for each one individually. Our report for the operation was as follows: *We attacked the primary target at 21.10 hrs from 20000ft, heading 083M at IAS 200. Bombed on green TI. Glow below cloud over very large area on leaving target. Large explosion centre of target area.*

The de-briefing team had the target films, which they recovered from each aircraft when it returned to the dispersal area. These films quite often provided them with considerable intelligence information as to where the bombs were dropped in relation to the actual designated Aiming Point (Bulls Eye in layman terms) or had the target even been hit. In all fairness to the crews, more often than not, their aircraft's photos would be of little or no value to the de-briefers, because the many explosions on the ground, or the heavy smoke from target fires would obscure the photo. The de-briefing also provided the team with information regarding enemy Luftwaffe fighter activity over the target as well as to or from, what ground defences we encountered and where, weather over the target, including to and from, and the accuracy of all aspects of the pre take off briefing. In conclusion, anything garnered from the actual sortie that would be of value for forthcoming operations.

F/O McManus and crew from 101 Squadron were one of the nine aircraft lost that night.

On our second trip, November 22, 1943, guess what Berlin! Having already completed a trip to Berlin, made this one marginally easier, I think. We did have some near misses by ack ack, which left proof of their accuracy with shrapnel holes in our fuselage.

On November 23, another planned Berlin operation, but we had to abort this one due to freezing rain, which created icing on the aircraft wings and propellers.

On November 26, the target was Stuttgart Germany. Just past Frankfurt, the bomber stream split into two groups. Some to Berlin and twenty- one Lancasters and one hundred and fifty seven Halifax bombers headed for Stuttgart. Once again, this was a manoeuvre to confuse the enemy fighters into splitting up their numbers in the Bomber stream.

Six Lancasters had taken off from Ludford Magna and only five returned.

CHAPTER SEVEN
THE FOURTH OPERATION

On December 2, 1943, once again our target was Berlin. We took off at 16.50 hours, one of twenty- one aircraft from Ludford Magna. We were to be part of a force of four hundred and fifty eight aircraft taking a direct route across the North Sea and Holland and directly to Berlin.

As we commenced our run into the target, Archie called "There's a Messerschmitt 110 tailing us Skip!" I replied, "Keep a sharp eye on him Archie as I'm on my bombing run." Archie said, "Oh, he's disappeared," I replied, "Watch for him because he may just be skirting away from the target area." We attacked the target at 20.30 hours at a height of twenty-one thousand feet, on a heading of 079 degrees and airspeed of two hundred nautical miles per hour. As we were on the final run into the target, and making several small heading adjustments for Bernie, just as he says "Bombs Away!" the aircraft made a severe lurch as we were hit by a flak-burst. It was almost simultaneous with the bomb release, and man it was a damn good near miss. It blew a hole through the dinghy installation on the starboard side, just outside the fuselage. We did not realize this until after we had landed. The aircraft filled with the smell of cordite, and almost immediately went into violent uncontrollable gyrations, which ended up in a very steep nose down attitude diving toward the centre of the fires blazing in the city below. I gave the order to the crew, to prepare to abandon aircraft. In the mean time, I struggled to regain control of the aircraft, and with judicious use of fifteen degrees of flap, small reductions of power, I slowly but surely regained control.

We had lost well over six thousand feet as a result of the ack ack strike but when I got it back on more or less on level flight, the elevator control seemed fairly normal. However, the aileron control was vibrating violently, and the port wing kept dropping. In order to keep the aircraft in level flight I had to keep my aileron control (on the stick) in a position similar to a ninety- degree steep turn to the starboard, and the severe vibration continued creating the impression that the control cable might break. If so, we would be doomed, as the aircraft would immediately roll over to the left and dive completely out of control, with little or no chance of anyone escaping. It was hard work keeping the aileron control hard right, and without John Rawcliffe's assistance, I never would have got the aircraft home.

In any event, it was decision time again. Bail out or try to get home. I felt that this was my decision alone, and very quickly I decided home we would go.

As I said before, to keep the aircraft level I had to keep the aileron control hard right as we were experiencing reduced lift on the port wing. In addition, the control column was still vibrating. I once again advised the crew to be prepared to bail out on short notice.

Archie yelled "Skip, that bastard Messerschmitt is back!" I called back " Archie, watch him because I'm having a hell of a time trying to keep this airplane level and no way can I take any evasive action!" "Okay Skip" All of a sudden all hell broke loose and Archie yells "He's after us! He's firing at us and I'm firing back!"

The Messerschmitt had six machine guns and four cannon all of which have tracer bullets in their weapon belts. Archie also has four guns firing back with tracers, creating quite a fireworks display around our airplane

All of a sudden, I hear oxygen bottles exploding and other racket associated with bullet impact! I could not take any evasive action and could only strive to keep the aircraft flying straight and level. Suddenly, Archie cried out, "I got the bastard; I got the bastard Skip! I got the bastard" and then suddenly everything went quiet.

It was time to ascertain what further damage had occurred during the attack. The flak hit some of our oxygen bottles and they exploded in the airplane. A machine gun bullet from the Messerschmitt went through, between my legs at crotch level, hit the steering pedestal, and ricocheted up through the windshield. Bullets came up between, the engineer and me, and we were sitting about ten inches apart.

After things settled down and I had things more or less under control, I asked for a report from all the stations. I started at the front end: "engineer?" "Okay skip, I'm fine", "bomb aimer?" "Okay skip, I'm fine, "navigator?" "Okay, skip," "radio operator?" "Okay Skip I'm fine," "mid upper turret?" and no answer. When I called the rear turret, there was again, no answer. I then assume, the gunners are hit and are seriously wounded or dead. I told John to put on the emergency oxygen bottle and check all stations. He discovered a wounded mid upper gunner, but Archie, the tail gunner seemed okay.

I was getting awfully tired trying to keep the aircraft level, with little or no help from the hydraulic system which controlled the ailerons, flaps and generally the complete steering mechanism. Again, I needed John's assistance in holding the control column. At one point, I warned the crew we might have to ditch in the channel as our fuel supply was running low. Corny came back with "Christ Skip, that's going to be a hell of a long way to swim!"

We limped all the way back to base, and as soon as we were able to contact the tower, I advised them of the critical situation we were experiencing and requested priority-landing clearance. The controller then gave me permission for a straight in approach. I tried lowering the flaps while still at four or five thousand feet. This manoeuvre exaggerated our wing heaviness problem so I decided to go around again. I advised the control tower I was "slightly shot up" and had serious control problems. As I came around the second time, I did not do any further altitude changing, just maintaining about four thousand feet until I was more or less lined up on the runway, which was a bit of a problem because I had so little control. I was just about to flare, at the same time cutting back on power. I had two and a half engines at this stage. One had totally quit and one was running extremely rough. All of a sudden, she (the controller) says, "B for Bravo, you haven't got your "nav" lights on!" At this point, I totally blew my cork. There was no one in the aircraft talking to me at this point. It was automatically "no talking" in this situation. I said, "you silly bitch! I told you I was slightly shot up!" (I was to find out later, the controller was the wife of a Squadron Leader navigator on our base's Mosquito squadron).

Well I got the plane onto the runway, I had little or no brakes, the hydraulics, as well were screwed, and I finally reached the end of the runway. After a rather gentle ground loop, I brought the aircraft to a full stop. The fire trucks and ambulances were there in a few minutes. In the meantime, we had a chance to look at a little bit of the damage. There was four feet missing off the port wing, and that is why she (the controller) could not see any navigation lights. The lights were gone! Approximately forty-eight square feet of the underside of the starboard wing was gone, two of our propellers had bullet holes in their blades and just outside the starboard side of the fuselage, there was now a large hole through the storage compartment of the dinghy, and obviously no dinghy. This is where the main blast had gone through. Lucky we did not have to ditch in the English Channel.

We evacuated the aircraft and after Archie finished kissing the pavement, we travelled by truck, back to the debriefing room.

We had a chance to talk to each other on the way, and then the whole story came out regarding Archie's battle with the Messerschmitt 110. With all the tracers from Archie's four guns and the Me110's four cannons and six guns, it looked like a fireworks display from the Fourth of July. After the attack was over, and Archie had nailed the Messerschmitt, I started the roll call for each station. The mid upper gunner had superficial wounds, and Archie said he had felt something running down his stomach inside his suit. The temperature was around minus thirty degrees centigrade but he took off his electric gloves anyway and unzipped his flying suit. He then put his hand inside his suit and discovered considerable wetness, which he believed must be blood. Then he discovered a hole in his stomach, which convinced him that he had been gut shot and was likely dying. Well when common sense overcame the panic, he realized the hole was his belly button, and the wetness, which he thought, was blood was sweat from the heat of battle.

Its fine to laugh about it now but remember this occurred after the fighter attacked and in the excitement poor Archie was sure he was dying of a gut shot.

The squadron awarded Archie a probable kill. Through the research of Dr. Theo Boiten of the Netherlands, author of the Nachtjagd War Diaries, I learned a Lt. Erich Rohrbach of 7/NJG5 had most probably attacked us. Rohrback's aircraft was shot down at Zepernik, north of Berlin that same night from return fire from a Lancaster. Rohrback died but both his crewmembers bailed out safely. I believe Archie should have been awarded a confirmed kill but unless someone in the bomber group had witnessed the incident, a gunner would only be awarded a probable.

The aircraft involved in this operation had to deal with clouds, high winds and when in the cloud, icing on the wings. It was a night-fighter's hey day for the enemy.

In the end, forty of our aircraft were missing including three from 101 Squadron. F/L Fraser-Hollins and F/S Murrell from "B" Flight, and S/L S.L. Robertson, DFC, from "C" Flight.

The station commander recommended me for an immediate award of the Distinguished Flying Medal, which I receive on January 4, 1944.

The station commander's remarks were as follows:

"Flight Sergeant Trotter, on the night in question, showed determination, skill and presence of mind worthy of high praise. Despite the perilous situation in which he was involved due to the

very serious damage to his starboard wing required the application of full port aileron to achieve level flight. He demonstrated a capacity for superb captaincy and airmanship by returning through the thickly infested fighter zones and defended areas between Berlin and the enemy coast and thereby undoubtedly saved his crew and much valuable equipment from destruction or from falling into the hands of the enemy. On reaching base, Flight Sergeant Trotter rose to the occasion, refrained from announcing his extremely damaged condition and remained patiently circling the aerodrome until other aircraft had landed safely. Finding that his aircraft became almost uncontrollable with engines throttled back, he calmly made a second attempt which proved successful. Subsequent inspection of the aircraft revealed damage of an outstanding severity and it is barely understandable how the aircraft retained any aerodynamic stability. I recommend that the commendable courage, calmness and presence of mind combined with very skilful airmanship shown by Flight Sergeant Trotter should be recognized by the immediate award of the D.F.M.

The formal citation, recorded in the London Gazette, January 7, 1944, read as follows:

*"**TROTTER,** Elmer John. Can/R.120945 Flight Sergeant, R.C.A.F., No. 101 Sqn. (immediate)*

Sorties 4, Flying hours 29.10 Pilot Air 2/5027

On the night of 2nd December, 1943, Flight Sergeant Trotter, a Canadian, was detailed to attack Berlin on his fourth operational sortie, having already attacked Berlin on two previous occasions. On the route out, having experienced difficult weather conditions, he arrived at the target and had just released his bombs when he was severely hit by anti-aircraft fire. The Lancaster was thrown *completely out of control and commenced to dive down onto the target. With magnificent coolness and presence of mind, Flight Sergeant Trotter ordered the crew to put on parachutes while he endeavoured to regain control. With expert skill and after losing considerable height, he managed to do this, only to find that he had scarcely any aileron control and no trimmers. His starboard mainplane had been shot to pieces aft the rear spar with three large holes inboard in between the outboard of his starboard engines. His mid-upper turret and compass were also unserviceable. His troubles were not over, however, for when leaving the target area and while trying to gain height, was attacked by an enemy night fighter which he successfully evaded after receiving further damage to the port outer engine. On his way back to base, he again ran into flak, but avoided being hit and he eventually made a safe landing at base. Flight Sergeant Trotter's outstanding ability and the magnificent coolness with which he controlled his aircraft undoubtedly saved it from destruction, while his superb captaincy in a critical situation inspired his crew with confidence. It is recommended that this N.C.O's splendid courage and determination be recognized by an immediate award of the D.F.M.*

8ᵗʰ December, 1943

Due to the severe damage suffered by our aircraft, (a cannon shot through one propeller and machine gun shot through another propeller) on top of all the other damage, the maintenance crew dismantled it, put it on a trailer, and sent it back to the AV Roe plant in Manchester. I think there was thirty five thousand staff at AV Roe, doing excellent workmanship under very trying circumstances.

The commanding officer informed me they were shipping the aircraft back to AV ROE, to be used as a monument for the recognition of the workmanship of their employees; and they would like me to come down and speak to their staff over the public address system. Well this was scarier than the operation itself, and I think they ended up taping an interview with me and putting that on the public address system. What a relief! Researching the history of that Lancaster, we found the aircraft had been rebuilt using parts from other aircraft; this was common practice when ever practical.

Very shortly thereafter, the commanding officer summoned me again, at which time he asked me if our crew would entertain a transfer to a Pathfinder Squadron. Knowing the Pathfinders were recognized as the "Elite of the Elite," I said, "I'd be really honoured to go to Pathfinders, but I'll have to obtain my crews' opinion first." He said, "Well I talked to Air Vice- Marshall Bennett, the Air Officer Commanding of 8 Group (Pathfinders), told him what you and your crew had accomplished while in 1 Group and he said they would be very pleased to have you." My crew agreed with me, and I passed on our unanimous decision to the CO.

We went on a one-week leave from December 9 to December 15 and on return to Ludford Magna, prepared for our transfer to Pathfinders.

My flying Assessment from Wing Commander Carey-Foster, Commanding Officer of 101 Squadron read *"As a L.B. pilot - Average Points in Flying or Airmanship which should be watched: - Average resolute and determined pilot.* The date was December 23, 1943. (I believe the reference to L.B. (light bomber) pilot is a typographical error and should have read H.B. for heavy bomber.

CHAPTER EIGHT

156(PFF) SQUADRON UPWOOD HUNTINGDONSHIRE

We Light The Way

On December 15, 1943, we reported for duty at 156 Squadron, PFF, Warboys. It was here we picked up a new Mid Upper Gunner, Walter Parfitt. Walter would be with us for the rest of our tour.

On January 7, 1944, our crew was on the battle order for an operation to Stettin, our first as a Pathfinder. Once we boarded the aircraft, we commenced our pre-flight check only to discover all our instruments were unserviceable, as was the rear turret. We had no recourse but to abort.

We had leave until January 13, so I took off for London on my 1000cc Sunbeam motorcycle. I stayed at the Regent Palace Hotel, which was the Canadian Forces favourite hotel. It became the place to go if you wanted to meet up with other Canadians. On this particular occasion, I failed to find anyone I knew, so I headed off to a pub, called Canada Place, about a quarter mile from the hotel. I was maybe halfway there when the air raid sirens started their mournful cry, and a Bobby quickly directed me to an air raid shelter, just a stone's throw away.

When I finally got into the place, it was crowded, almost body-to-body. I was only there a few minutes when a female voice behind me said "hello Canada." I turned around and found a very attractive young woman who said, "Hello, my name is Angela." I responded with my name and we continued with conversation about the war, the bombing raids, and so forth. She was wearing coveralls with the word "Warden" stamped on the back in big letters. As well, she had a gas mask and an Army helmet, which left me with no doubt as to her responsibilities. She then told me she was just off shift and was on her way home, when she took refuge in this shelter as the sirens sounded. She asked how long I had been in Britain and was I a pilot. I also noticed that she was wearing a wedding ring, and I inquired in what branch of the services was her husband was serving. She told me he lost his life in the Dieppe landings. I stumbled out my sincere regrets, and put my arm around her shoulders as she appeared about to cry. She quickly mustered control of her emotions, apologized, and carried on with a general conversation.

When the all clear siren sounded, there was a steady rush to leave the shelter. I asked, "How far do you have to go, would you like me to see you home?" Angela replied," it is very nice of you to offer, but you must have other plans." I assured her I had nothing planned and would be pleased to see her home.

Her house was about a half mile away, and when we arrived, I bid her good night and turned to leave. She asked me if I would like to come up for a cup of tea. That sounded like a good idea and I want to assure the sceptics I had no evil intentions. We must have talked for two or three hours and I decided to take my leave. I asked her for a cab telephone number, and she told me at that time of the night I would have difficulty getting one. She said she had a guest bedroom, which I was welcome to use, and then I could go back to my hotel in the morning. Her suggestion made sense so I accepted her offer. Shortly thereafter, I retired, and after the long day was soon sound asleep. I do not know how long I slept before I awakened to a naked body sliding into bed with me. The rest of the night is history. Suffice to say, the next morning I whistled all the way back to my hotel. I never realized what I had been missing.

On January 20, 1944, the briefing was for another attack on Berlin. Again, we had to abort as our navigator became ill with vomiting and nearly passed out. I told him that there was no way we could continue with him having his air sickness problem, I also told him we all felt he was a very capable navigator, and he was well liked by all of our crew, but his unpredictable air sickness problem posed a real flight safety problem for the whole crew including himself. He agreed and I immediately asked our Squadron Commander, S/L Dickie Walbourne for a replacement. He whole-heartedly agreed, and shortly thereafter introduced me to an Australian Squadron Leader, Barcroft (Bart) Melrose Mathers, whom he highly recommended.

When I asked Bart if he would consider joining our crew, it was at once obvious by his enthusiasm, that I had made a good choice. Our whole crew quickly accepted Bart. Our new navigator had already completed one tour (a minimum of thirty operations) and wanted badly to get back into the fray. So much so, that he took a reduction in rank to do so. Despite his obvious experience, he melded in with our whole crew quickly and enthusiastically, sharing his prior experiences quietly and in an unassuming manner. This however was his first experience with Pathfinders, but I had no doubt that with his background, he would quickly prove well qualified as a PFF navigator.

January 21, our target was Magdeburg and we were assigned a supporter role, obviously to give me a chance to evaluate Bart's ability as a Pathfinder navigator. A supporter dropped window in addition to carrying a full bomb load. The window dropped en route to the target was supposed to confuse the German radar operators into believing there were more bombers in the raid than there actually were.

Sixteen of the twenty-one Lancasters from our squadron took off commencing at 20:00 hours to form part of the six hundred and forty eight aircraft making the first major raid on this city. We arrived over the target at 22:54 hours and met with heavy fighter activity, which soon took its toll.

One of those lost was Flight Lieutenant Kilvington and his crew. Later, we learned the crew had been captured and taken as prisoners of war.

On January 27, it was off to Berlin again as a supporter. We took off at 00:10 hours carrying a bomb load of four, one thousand pounders, and eleven five hundred pound bombs. On this mission, Sgt. Webb joined us as our Mid Upper gunner. We were to form part of a group of five hundred and fifteen Lancasters. Once again, cloud obscured the target.

Thirty- three Lancasters were lost, but this time, none from 156 Squadron.

At this point, we were lucky enough to have a little over two-week's stand-down due primarily to bad weather.

On February 10, King George VI, Queen Elizabeth, and Princess Elizabeth visited the airbase. I was lucky enough to be seated two seats down from Princess Elizabeth and almost across the table from the Queen during the lunch. My problem was I was so nervous I could hardly eat. The King appeared to be quite shy and seemed to have a speech impediment; on the other hand, the Queen was most impressive in every aspect.

February 15 it was back on the battle order. Flight Sergeant Fitzhenry joined us as Navigator and Sgt. Felstead stood in for our Engineer. Bart and John were grounded for medical reasons, flu or bad colds. Twenty- one Lancasters took off starting at 20:00 hours from 156 Squadron. Six of us were to join up with eighteen others for a spoof raid on Frankfurt-on-Oder. Our purpose was to lure fighters away from the main force, headed to Berlin. The eight hundred and ninety one aircraft involved made this one of the largest forces ever dispatched on any operation.

The spoofer diversion was determined to be unsuccessful and forty- three aircraft were lost including Flight Lieutenant M.C Stimpson DFC and crew from 156 Squadron.

The role of the spoofer on any raid was to create confusion in the Luftwaffe Fighter Control organization as to what our main target was to be. In other words, the spoofer was to draw the fighters away from our Main Bomber force. If your role has been successful, the spoofer losses would be higher but the main force losses would be considerably lower enabling the dropping of a much greater bomb tonnage on the primary target.

On February 19, with our new navigator and Sergeant Moss filling in as Flight Engineer, we were assigned as a Primary marker on our target Leipzig. This meant we were to drop coloured flares identifying the target aiming point. We took off at 23:54 in light falling snow, carrying about seven thousand pounds of bombs, and our scheduled arrival on target was 03:59. The forecast was for strong to severe head winds but actually ended up as light northerly winds and eighty percent cloud cover.

Twenty-one aircraft left 156 Squadron to comprise a part of the main force totalling eight hundred and twenty three aircraft. We encountered heavy enemy fighter activity all the way to the target and primarily due to the incorrect wind forecast; many of the bombers arrived at the target before H hour (their scheduled drop time). They were required to circle while waiting for the first Pathfinders to mark the target aiming point. Any time you had to circle a target inevitably resulted in more aircraft lost to enemy fighters and ground defences.

Seventy-Eight aircraft were lost that night including Squadron Leader A.D. Saunders, Warrant Officer R. Stanners and their crews of 156 Squadron.

February 20 our target was Stuttgart, with our crew assigned as the primary blind marker. This type of target marking, done by radar, is required when cloud cover obscures the target, and meant the Pathfinder navigators would have to calculate, very accurately, the wind speed and the drift for the parachute markers. The markers would be dropped in different colour configurations hopefully known only to our bombers, and would provide a target aiming point above the clouds. These markers had to be replaced by the Pathfinder crews designated "Backer Uppers" throughout the attack as they had a burn out time, as well as a drift distance time. This type of target marking required very accurate radar provided by H2S, and later as they came on stream, the more effective

H2X system, which allowed large targets with rivers, lakes, or bays, to stand out more distinctly on the radar screen.

We took off at 00:14 carrying nine thousand pounds of bombs along with flares and TIs (coloured flares called Target Indicators). We encountered thick cloud and moderate to severe icing, plus heavy fog over the target area which, made night fighter attack difficult, however there was a lot of flak.

Of the five hundred and ninety eight aircraft deployed for this mission, ten were lost, including Flight Lieutenant D.K. MacKay DFC a Canadian and his crew, which included Squadron Leader Muir who was the Squadron's gunnery leader, and had filled in as the rear gunner that night.

February 24 our target was Schweinfurt, Germany's main ball bearing factories. Our job was Primary blind marker. While the target was clear, searchlights lit up the sky and there was heavy flak. Seven hundred and thirty four aircraft carried out this first attack by Bomber Command on this city. We were to attack in two waves, separated by a two-hour interval, which was something new to us.

A total of thirty-three aircraft and crews were lost on this raid including, three of the crews from 156 Squadron: Wing Commander E.F. Porter, Pilot Officer S.W.G. Neighbour and Flight Lieutenant J.A. Day.

Upon returning from this sortie, I was looking forward to a much needed, one-week leave. John and I drove to Preston in Lancashire to stay with his family.

I had just purchased the pride of my motorcar life, a beautiful red, Singer Le Mans 4 seat convertible. The hood itself was about nine feet long, and it was so long ago I am not sure what the actual horsepower was. I do know I got very poor mileage on a tank of petrol, which I am sure, was the reason I was able to purchase it at such a low price. I think I paid around five hundred pounds or twenty five hundred Canadian dollars. All I know is with all the crew pitching in with their fuel rations, and a good deal of scrounging, I could drive about fifty or sixty kilometres per month. In addition, our ground crew always seemed to find a gallon or two of petrol each month, which they gladly donated to a good cause.

I had been to the Rawcliffes' before but once again, the welcome was rather overwhelming. John's parents were wonderful people. It seemed they knew at least half of the Preston citizenry, and had set a goal for me to meet half of the ones they knew. I always felt at home there, and the time spent with them took away some of my longing for my own family.

After we had been shot down, Mrs. Rawcliffe wrote to my mother telling her how I had sung the Maple Leaf Forever for them and had told stories of Canada and my family. She spoke only as one mother could to another mother, of their love for their sons and their hopes for a quick reunion. Even today, reading her letter brings tears to one's eyes.

On March 15, we took off at 19:27, into forecasted heavy head winds, carrying a twenty thousand pound bomb load; we were one of twenty-four aircraft from 156 Squadron. Our target was Stuttgart. We were once again a Primary Blind Marker and one of eight hundred and sixty three aircraft assigned to this raid.

We flew across France, almost to Switzerland before we turned to approach the target. We encountered heavy fighter activity, which destroyed several of our aircraft in the target area. We identified the target at 23:16 from eighteen thousand feet and dropped the first TIs about four minutes later. At about 20:39 hours and still at eighteen thousand feet, we saw another aircraft blow up, before he had dropped his bombs, obviously a direct hit. Our crew saw no survivors nor did we expect otherwise. On return to our base, we reported that the raid seemed to spread to the west over a very large area.

All twenty-four aircraft from 156 returned safely home that night. The last time twenty-four left and returned safely was July 24, 1943.

March 18 we were the first of the twenty- four squadron aircraft to take off at 19:16 hours en route to Frankfurt, as Primary blind marker. We were part of the eight hundred and forty aircraft on this sortie. We encountered German fighters just before reaching the target; however, cloud cover provided a fair bit of protection from them,

Twenty-two aircraft were lost, but all our crews from 156 Squadron, made it home safely once again.

On March 22, we were off to Frankfurt again, this time as the Blind Backer Upper. The Blind Backer Uppers are spaced throughout the raid and given specific times to drop markers on existing markers, or as directed by the Master Bomber to ensure the original target remained correctly marked.

We took off at 18:47 along with twenty other aircraft from the base and joined up with the main bomber force now comprised of eight hundred and sixteen aircraft. We again took an indirect route over the Dutch coast before turning south to the target. According to Bomber Command records, this along with a diversionary raid to Kiel confused the Germans for some time, and as a result, we encountered only a few fighters. The attack was a major success and according to the Frankfurt Diary, the raids of March 18, 22 and 24 dealt "the worst and most fateful blow of the war to Frankfurt, a blow which simply ended the existence of the Frankfurt which had been steadily built up since the middle ages."

On 24 March, twenty- one aircraft left base for Berlin. We took off at 18:59 once again assigned the role of Blind Backer Up. We joined up with eight hundred and ten others to form an aircraft group. Bomber Command called this night "the night of the strong winds." The winds were extremely strong from the North, so much so, the bomber stream became scattered and the winds blew many aircraft off course. In addition, the winds severely affected the marking.

Seventy- two aircraft were lost with fifty of them believed to be destroyed by flak.

We lost Flight Lieutenant T.R. Richmond and his crew this night, and this would be the last major raid on Berlin by the RAF.

On March 30, 1944 we took part in what was the soon to become the infamous raid on Nuremberg. It was to be our last sortie with 156 Squadron. This particular night earned the name of "Killer Moon Night" from the aircrews, as there would be a full moon, making us sitting ducks for German ground defences and more importantly, their night fighters. Even though the weather forecast indicated we would have cloud cover en route to the target, it was clear sky all the way, and the full moon only served to enhance the Luftwaffe night fighter threat. They had a "hey day!" With no cloud cover over the target, the anti aircraft defences were able to bring all of their guns and search lights into action visually. What a nightmare! We witnessed the destruction of numerous aircraft, primarily by the night fighters.

Searchlights were one of the biggest fears of crews, and in particular, of "being coned" over the target. The Master Searchlight is blue and radar controlled. When it suddenly came on, it immediately was on a target, and several manually operated lights would then join it thus visually coning the Master Searchlight's target. If you were unfortunate enough to be the coned individual, you would be a sitting duck for the night fighters. However, a more dangerous situation was suddenly developing in your cockpit because of the coning. The candlepower of several searchlights on your aircraft is unbelievable! They created a brilliance factor within the cockpit, blinding you, and making it impossible to read the instrument panel. I believe this resulted in many pilots losing control of their aircraft, and thus they and their crew became another statistic. I remember only once being coned, and being completely blinded followed by a terrible adrenaline surge. I believe this resulted in me inadvertently rolling the Lancaster. The Lancaster is not an aerobatic aircraft, and to survive a roll at night while blinded by searchlights would seem to indicate that God or one of his deputies was my co-pilot on the night in question.

We took off at 22:29 designated as a Blind Backer Up. Twenty aircraft from 156 joined the group, of seven hundred and seventy five others. Many fighter forces harassed us all the way to the target, and again on the route home. Back in England, we met with a heavy snowstorm and eleven of the 156 aircraft force landed at other bases. With ninety-six aircraft lost, eighty-two of them en route to the target (over ten percent) and fourteen on the return home plus a further forty-five in crash landings in Britain, due primarily to severe inclement weather at the home bases. This was by far the heaviest loss experienced by Bomber Command in World War II.

Our Squadron lost four aircraft and crews that night, Captain F. Johnson, Warrant Officer J.A. Murphy, Pilot Officer L. Lindley and Squadron Leader P.R. Goodwin and their crews.

If you were able to put all one hundred and forty one of the Lancasters wing tip to wing tip, they would cover a distance of 3.63 miles, and their crews would total over one thousand men.

Many people ask how we reacted to the enormous losses of human life. To try this exercise in futility is difficult to say the least. However, I will give my best shot to find an answer as to why in my short life span I appear to be apathetic to the very existence of danger and or death.

In Bomber Command, in particular the Pathfinder Force, our survival rate on a tour of forty- five operations tour was a very meagre three to four percent yet neither I, or my crew ever discussed the dismal figures. On every sortie, we would associate with death at least two or three times and other than a "that was a close one" comment, we resumed the norm very quickly. When we sat down for our breakfast and saw the empty table normally occupied by "Jones" and his crew, generally a member of the crew would say "Looks like Jonesy and his crew got the chop" and that would be the end of the conversation.

This may sound cold blooded to the uninitiated however; one must remember we volunteered for this job, fully accepting the well-known casualty lists associated with it. Furthermore, we were well aware if any one of us were to dwell on the survival aspect we could become a serious hazard not only to ourselves individually, but more importantly to our crew as a whole.

I certainly do not suggest we believed we were any more courageous than the other crews were, nor did we consider ourselves infallible. I do believe we worked extra hard to be professionally proficient and hoped that Lady Luck would give us a better than average break. Somebody had to be in the three to four percent number who survived and we believed we were well qualified to be there.

CHAPTER NINE
ENTERTAINMENT

People often ask what we did to occupy ourselves during stand-downs, after operations and such. I must admit I was not a big fan of the Mess. Military regulations dictated as officers, we were segregated from those of our crew who were Non Commissioned Officers. I have previously said, these boys were my brothers, my only family on this side of the ocean, and we cared deeply for each other. Therefore, it would stand to reason, we would like to spend our downtime together and have fun as a family.

We often times would ride our bicycles to the nearest pub where we would consume several pints of beer and play darts. Every pub and mess in Britain had several dartboards, and I think it was their most popular pastime. I became a relatively good dart player, but I must admit it cost me a fair amount of money to reach the standard required to hold my own. I believe most British males were born with a set of darts in their fist, and certainly, during the war they just loved to find a Colonial (Canadian) who wanted to learn how to play the game. As I said, the education cost was quite high.

On those occasions when I did attend the mess, it would be the usual tipping of a few alcoholic beverages, singing around the piano, usually off colour songs, general conversations, and wrist twisting. We also played a lot of bridge and I became quite proficient at the game. Of course, there were the inevitable horseplay games. Some of the ones I remember are as follows:

The "Runway" game consists of taking pie plates filled with water, and a lit candle in each. These would be placed in two separate lines down the middle of the floor with about four or five feet between the rows. We would then take a seat cushion and hold it to our chest, take off at a run, dive headfirst and slide on the cushion as far as we could go without crashing into the pie plates. We were usually quite inebriated and I am amazed there were no fires.

In another game similar to runway, we would take the chesterfields and line them up in a row with the backs facing inward. The next step was to take a broom handle put the handle end in your armpit, and reach down as far as you could with a straight arm. The spot where the tip of your middle finger touched the handle was the marking point for your hands to hold the broom. You would then bring the handle and your hands up to your nose, tip your head back and look to the ceiling. Making sure you keep the end of the broom handle pointed at a spot on the ceiling, two fellows would turn you around and around, face you towards the runway and tell you to drop the broom and try to make it down the row of chesterfields. Of course your equilibrium is totally out of whack as is your semicircular canal and after dropping the broom, you would be severely off balance and falling to the right as you tried to run down the runway, banging into the furniture until you would finally fall over. This of course would get all the guys with their egos going, saying; "I can do that, no problem!" Of course, they could not, but it would make for a lot of laughter.

The other game I remember well was "Poop (polite word) the "tator" (Potato)". We would position three or four chesterfields like a hurdle course with about five paces between them. The contestant would then take a billiard ball and tuck it up in his crotch. He cannot touch the ball with his hand(s) or any other aid until game is finished, unless he has fouled out, in which case he must return to the start line and start over. The purpose of the game is to travel as quickly as possible, climbing over each chesterfield while keeping the billiard ball in place. After making it over the last chesterfield, the contestant must proceed to a bucket located on the floor, squat over it and drop the ball into the bucket. If he dropped the ball before reaching the bucket, or if he missed the bucket while trying to drop his ball in it, he must go back to the start position and start over.

Another little game when you had rookies in the mess was to bet them they could not stand on their heads for a full three minutes. It was in the rules that you would help them get into the proper position, with one of their buddies holding each leg, and then when the victim states that he is ready to have the timing begin, you let go of his legs. At the same time, you and another conspirator pour a pint of beer down each leg of the victim's pants. Guaranteed you win your bet every time.

All of the above included a fair amount of gambling, which was quite common on the bases.

CHAPTER TEN

582 SQUADRON
LITTLE STAUGHTON

"Provolanius designante" (We Fly Before Marking)

On April 1, 1944 "C" Flight from 156 Squadron Upwood, Huntingdonshire and another flight from 7 Squadron from Oakington were put together to form 582 Squadron, a new Pathfinder Squadron to be based at Little Staughton in Bedfordshire. Number 109 Mosquito Squadron joined us the following day.

Our first call to the 582 Squadron Battle Order was on April 24. The target was Karlsruhe, and we were to be the Blind Backer Upper. The weather was clear and we encountered very little enemy opposition.

On April 27, we were off to Friedrichshaven a small town with several factories known for manufacturing aircraft gearboxes for German tanks and other equipment. We did not notice any interceptions by Luftwaffe night fighters on the route into the target, despite the bright moonlight, but once we got there, the sky was loaded with them.

Friedrichshaven was a difficult target requiring great accuracy in marking and bombing in that, it was located on Lake Constance and Switzerland was only about twenty- five kilometres across the lake.

There were three hundred and twenty two aircraft involved in this very successful sortie, with all vital factories destroyed.

We lost eighteen Lancasters this night including our Commanding Officer of 156 Squadron, Wing Commander E.C. Eaton DFC, and his crew; so soon; we had hardly gotten to know him.

May 7 to 19th, our concentration was on aircraft factories and railway yards in an effort to slow down the German Transportations System. The highlight for me was receiving my Temporary Pathfinder Badge on May 7and Bernie Pullin, my bomb aimer receiving his Commission to Pilot Officer also in May, in recognition of his performance.

On the night of May 24 /25th, the operation was the Aachen West Marshalling Yards. Our crew was on stand down that night but my friend and fellow Canadian F/L Stuart W. Little, DFC. "Sammy" and his crew were on the Battle Order. They took off at 0020 hours but failed to return with the rest of the Squadron. The crew, were reported as MIA (Missing in action). How we hated that acronym.

I first met Sammy at 156 Squadron along with F/L John Hewitt. The three of us became very good friends, and took turns volunteering when required for various sorties. John and I took the loss of Sammy quite hard, and I am sure the rest of the Squadron felt the same, given his experience and successful completion of over thirty sorties.

June 6, 1944 D-Day

The Bomber Crews had known for some time that a huge operation was in the planning stages. We did not know when it would take place or what the operation would be; we just knew it was coming. It was at a briefing on this day, that the magnitude and details of "Operation Overlord were made known to us.

We were assigned bombings runs from Cherbourg to Le Havre. I remember the sky filled with aircraft, like wall-to-wall carpeting, and the channel covered with ships. The trips were of very short duration, and oft times we refuelled and reloaded, and were quickly briefed on another target.

This operation introduced us to a new phrase, "Bomb Line." This extremely important term passed from the Army invasion forces to the Air force hierarchy, and thence to the various Squadrons involved in supplying close air support to the Army's advancing Invasion Forces. Theoretically, the bomb line was to give us a geographic line that represented the ground forces maximum allowable forward incursion into enemy territory, at any designated time. I said theoretically, because some times in the heat of battle, some army units might suddenly have a breakthrough on the enemy's lines, or have the enemy retreating, and their natural reaction would be to keep them retreating. In the meantime, they had crossed the Bomb Line, and to make a long story short, there were times when they could or would be victims of the Air Force Close Support bombing.

I have, post war, asked numerous Army Officers or NCOs, if they had ever been victims of such attacks, and some said they heard of incidents, but normally it was brought to their attention in briefings, when they were warned of the terrible consequences, that might occur if they violated the "Bomb Line."

On June 14, the target for our operation was the Douai Locomotive Works. My good friend and one of our notorious three regular volunteers, F/Lt. J. H. Hewitt, DFC "John" was designated the Master Bomber.

We took off at 0021 and the Master Bomber followed three minutes later. Our crew were designated as the Illuminator for this raid. We identified the target using H2S and the target was marked with green TI's. The weather was 6-8/10ths cloud, based at ten thousand feet and visibility was moderate and hazy. We attacked at 0156 hours from ten thousand feet. We dropped twenty- four seven inch hooded yellow flares, which really lit up the whole target area, including the canals and built up area. At 0157 hours, we dropped our bombs. The green markers lay on track about five hundred yards apart and red TI's fell on top of each other midway between the greens. Bombing concentrated on TIs as instructed by the Master Bomber.

This was the last anyone heard from him. We were later told by the Squadron Commander, John's aircraft, was intercepted by a night fighter over Douai, and crashed, killing all aboard. Two were now gone from our Three Musketeers. Two of my best friends, now I was the only one left of the three-some; I felt awful, very blue to-day, as did my crew.

Archie and I took advantage of a thirty-six hour pass and headed out to London, which was about forty-five miles from the base.

We were at the Trianon Ballroom the night the Germans launched their first all night V1 Rocket attack on London. June 15/16, 1944.The Brits practiced the saying of the "stiff upper lip" in many ways, not the least of which "the show must go on" in their entertainment world. When Archie and I decided to return to our hotel, the V1s were exploding regularly and we wondered if they might be like the Japanese "kamikaze" suicide pilots. Undaunted, we waved down a cab and returned to our hotel, the famous Regent Palace, the Canadian "warriors" favourite hotel.

The next morning, I decided I would enjoy the luxury of a barbershop shave. As we headed off to the recommended barbershop, we noticed that the bomb explosions were widely separated, and appeared to be tapering off. We had questioned some of the hotel staff as well as a Bobby, and it was obvious no one really knew what actual form the bombings were taking.

We arrived at the Barber Shop, the only customers I might add. The barber greeted us very warmly, and as I seated myself in the chair, he immediately asked us, because we were Military I assume, what we thought the Jerries (Germans) were up to. We had to admit, that we knew just as little as he did.

The barber placed wet heated towels upon my face, and never quit talking, mostly about his speculations as to what the Germans were trying to do to his city. Just as he started to wield his straight razor down my neck, a terrific explosion occurred close enough to his shop to crack two of his windows. As he stood over me, with razor poised and hand violently shaking, he said; "I say matey, that one was damned close!" I responded, "You think it was close from your position, well I assure you, it was a hell of a lot closer from mine!" I learned a very good lesson. Never have a shave when a bomb attack is taking place.

Archie and I left the barber- shop and wandered around looking at the damage the city had sustained from the many bombing raids over the past couple of years. We came around a corner and almost immediately, on our right side, a large area between two buildings had been cordoned off. A Bobby, an English police officer was patrolling the area and I asked him what the reason was for the area being out of bounds. He told us there was an unexploded bomb approximately two hundred yards from where we were standing, and there was a Canadian Bomb expert trying to disarm it. I asked if we could go in to see what was happening, to which he replied with an emphatic "NO." He immediately turned his back, and hands clasped behind his back, proceeded to walk away from us. This we took as a "if you are dumb enough to go in, be my guest."

We ducked under the warning tape and ran until we came upon a large crater. There, straddling a two thousand pound bomb was a Canadian Army Major with a cigarette dangling from his mouth. I cannot remember his name but he became almost a household hero in Britain. He waved at us and continued working on the bomb. I turned to Archie and said; "Boy does he have guts. If he makes one little mistake, he will be history." Suddenly it dawned on us. We were sitting on the edge of the crater a mere, twenty, or thirty feet from him! We took off running and as we reached the street, the Bobby shook his finger at us, not unlike the way you would at a youngster who had been a bad boy. We left the site with the Bobby's laughter echoing in our ears.

During this period of the invasion, all crews had to remain on base and on alert. We often were scrambled with very short briefings. We spent the last week of June, concentrating on the destruction of the German rocket plane installations and railway yards located in the Pas de Calais area, there-by disrupting the German transportation system, and especially the V1 rocket assaults on Britain.

Suddenly on June 30, the CO summoned fourteen crews to what appeared to be an emergency briefing. Our CO informed us that Hitler's 2nd and 9th Panzer divisions were converging at a road junction at Villers Bocage. Their goal was to attack the British and American Armies in Normandy. There were to be two hundred and sixty six aircraft involved with Squadron Leader B.W. MacMillan of 582 Squadron taking on the role of Master Bomber.

We took off at 1836 hours. The Master Bomber identified the target at 1959 hours. On the approach to the target, MacMillan repeated instructions to the main force to come in at four thousand feet. We did not hear those instructions and at 1956 hours saw the first red Tis. We heard instructions to the main force to bomb these with a two-second overshoot, and attacked at 20:00 hours from ten thousand feet. We heard no further instructions due to interference on the radio. At 2003 hours, a load of green TIs was seen, close to the aiming point, which was now obliterated by smoke. We learned upon return to base only about fifty aircraft heard the Master bomber's instructions to bomb at four thousand feet, as a result most of the main bomber force came in at fourteen thousand feet. Showers of bombs from those above forced the fifty to take evasive action to avoid being struck by those same bombs. F/O H.G.Hall was hit by flak on the underside of the port main plate, severing the petrol line to the port outer engine, and had to land at Thorney Island. Overall, the attack was deemed a success, and the planned

Panzer attack did not take place. When we saw our aiming point photo, we could see one lone tank trying to make a getaway. Too bad Tiger!

We had a few days off for rest and relaxation and took off for some playtime. We returned to Little Staugton and soon realized that July was to be a very busy month.

From July 2 to the 15[th,] we flew seven sorties attacking rocket plane installations, and factories manufacturing aircraft and tank parts. All were located in France and all were daylight operations. All were very successful.

On July 18, we flew two operations. In the morning at 0440 hours, we took off for Cagny. This was to be a daylight tactical attack. We attacked at 0621 hours from eight thousand feet. The weather over the target area was no cloud and unlimited visibility. At 0618 hours, we could hear the Master Bomber instructing the bombers to bomb red TIs, and overshoot one width (approximately two hundred yards). The bombing was very well concentrated. We returned to base and landed at 0730 hours.

On both of our missions on this date, we could not have our regular aircraft, (F) for Freddy because of minor maintenance problems. We also were without Archie who had crossed swords with the Base Commander, and naturally, he did not win. The CO summoned me his office and briefed me accordingly. The Orderly Room Sergeant filled me in as to the details.

Apparently our Archie, after having one or two too many in the Sergeants mess, was walking back to his barracks, when the CO drove by in his Staff car with his CO flag prominently displayed on the cars bonnet. Station Standing Orders were explicit throughout ALL British and Commonwealth Military establishments, all military personnel will salute the CO's staff car when his flag is displayed. In any event, obviously Archie did not comply, and when the CO had his driver back up and summon Archie over to his car, he admonished our rear gunner of his not complying with the standard orders. Archie had often stated to anyone who was prepared to listen, "I'm here to fight Hitler not to be on parade." Archie in this case was not content to just apologize, button up his uniform, straighten his hat, salute the CO, and probably come away with a couple of days as extra duty Orderly Sergeant. No not our Archie! Archie is not yet done; he now proceeded to tell the CO "my skipper has more guts in his little finger than you have in your whole body." Boy oh boy, in WW1 he would likely have earned a spot in front of a firing squad. Instead, he was immediately placed "On Charge," and sent under escort to a severe Disciplinary Centre for twenty- one days.

On his return to our crew, Archie told us, the daily routine at the centre started at 0500 hrs, with his first job, cleaning up his cell, which included shining his floor until it was spotless. This was followed with marching back and forth on the parade square with a hundred pound pack on his back and a rifle on his shoulder for one hour. On the completion of this exercise, he was allowed to shower followed by a very basic breakfast. Then it was back to his cell only to discover that the great job of cleanup, which he had completed first thing in the morning, was now an absolute mess with the floor covered with mud etc, and he had to start all over again. I wonder who ruined his nice cleaning job.

On our second trip on July 18, I garnered the responsibility of master bomber on a daylight attack on the Vaires Marshalling Yards in Paris. This time, we had another new experience.

Another Lancaster and crew were assigned to be my protector against attack from enemy fighter aircraft.

Squadron Leader Alabaster, the Captain of the assigned aircraft, was a recent addition to 582 Squadron and had completed a tour of thirty operations as a navigator. He had gone to an RAF Flight Training School, received his Pilot's wings, and was now starting his second tour. His instructions from the Squadron Operation Officer, was to fly loose formation on my aircraft, with his crew's eyes providing additional warning of enemy fighter activity, and in the event of an enemy attack, doubling our fire- power against the attacker. The theory was great as I would be extremely busy directing the main bomber force, which encompassed one hundred and ten aircraft.

We took off at 1605 hours. The weather over the target was clear with a slight haze and moderate visibility; I could visually identify the target. At 1725 hours when crossing the coast at Dieppe, I instructed the main force to watch timing as the attack seemed likely to start early. At 1732 hours I decided that the main force could not be held back sufficiently so we went ahead to mark. At 1746 hours, I called the Deputy Master, and held him back for a while and then told him to bomb. We both bombed together with the Deputy's down just before ours. I could see that the yellow TI's were right on the aiming point so I then instructed the main force to bomb on the yellow TI's.

The bombing at first was only fair. I then instructed the main force to bomb more accurately and the concentration became noticeably much better. Red TI's fell at 1756 hours south of the marshalling yards but were indistinguishable on the ground. At 1757 hours, second reds fell slightly southwest of the marshalling yards and another lot of reds fell next to the village southeast of the yards. I issued instructions to ignore these last reds. F/L Alabaster was directly behind me and bombed as Bernie released our bombs. He reported at debriefing that he could hear no instructions from me until after the bombing.

Upon leaving the target area, I went into my usual corkscrew routine. This means the pilot would make a diving turn to left for approximately five hundred feet, allowing his airspeed to build up, followed by a climbing turn to the right co-incident with a significant increase in power. After exceeding the original altitude by approximately five hundred feet, plus or minus one to two hundred feet, commence a rolling dive again to the left. It is very important that you do not repeat the same manoeuvre, too often as the Luftwaffe pilots will just sit and wait for you to make an excellent target.

I apologise for being repetitive in describing the corkscrew however this manoeuvre was our main defensive tactic, enhancing our chances of survival

To the uninitiated, this modus operandi appeared relatively simple, however, in real life, when I commenced an un-announced corkscrew, S/L Alabaster would have been, very hard pressed to stay in "loose" formation with me. Lancaster pilots would have no difficulty understanding where I am coming from, but for non-heavy bomber pilots and certainly non-pilots, suffice to say with the Lancaster, even with limited hydraulic assisted controls, it was a real heavy-duty physical workout to execute a proper corkscrew. For a pilot even to fly a loose formation during such a manoeuvre, well, all I could say was "Wow!"

In any event, during our de-briefing after our return to base, S/L Alabaster was still dripping wet from perspiration. I could not begin to come up with enough accolades to express my respect for this pilot. We believed the attack to be a success. There were one hundred and ten aircraft involved.

I believe by giving instructions to move the aiming point, we were able to systematically destroy the vast majority of the rail traffic in the Marshalling Yard with simple instructions such as "Bomb load this is the Eagle, move your aiming point three hundred yards north of the green markers, I say again" and I would repeat my instructions.

On July 20, we took off at 2000 hours as the Deputy Master Bomber. Our target was Ferme de Forestal. Again, Archie was not with us and F/S Jacobs flew in his place. The weather over the target included patches of fog. We were carrying six 1000lb bombs plus numerous yellow target indicators. At 2120 hours, we were advised basement fourteen thousand five hundred feet. (Basement means the cloud base). Two reds were to be seen cascading at 2130hours. These fell on the corner of the target to the SW. Further loads of reds fell just NE of the target. At 2133 hours, we visually identified the aiming point and attacked from fourteen thousand feet, heading 096 degrees 155 knots. We dropped Yellows between the two reds across the target. At 2137 hours, the Master Bomber gave instructions to bomb between Red and Yellows.

2138 hours he corrected it to bomb left of Yellow TI and kept repeating it. Then his last instructions were to bomb Yellows. The Bombing was concentrated and the aiming point was completely covered.

The boys and I left for two weeks leave from July 24 to August 6.

Archie and I took the train up to Garmouth, in Morayshire, Scotland, to visit his parents and sister, Margaret.

From our first greeting, I felt like one of the family. It was, to say the least one of the best leaves I had since arriving in Britain.

I remember Mr. Archibald taking me out deer hunting one afternoon. Although we did not even sight a deer, we did have a wonderful four hours in the beautiful countryside. It was obvious how much he and his wife loved their son. I felt lonesome for my own Mom and Dad and wondered how much longer it would be before I saw them again.

The eight days I spent in Garmouth went by far too quickly. With no air raid sirens or other wartime noises, it was hard to believe we were at war. When it was time to leave, the out-pouring of tears, hugs and kisses soon brought me back to reality. I promised them I would take good care of their boy and that we would be back to see them when our double tour leave came up.

Little did I know what the future held for us in just a few days, and that this would be the last time these beautiful people would see their only son.

From Garmouth, I headed to Lancashire to spend some time with John and his family. It was here I, was introduced to a very good friend of theirs, a well-known, professional artist E.Robinson. Mr. Robinson's son was also in the air force and had been reported missing in January. For some reason, he said I reminded him of his son, and asked if I would sit and allow him to paint my portrait. My first thought was "What on my leave!"

I resisted as best I could, but John's mother intervened and said it would make such a lovely gift for my mother who I had told her was not well. This swayed me and I sat for fifteen to twenty minutes a day for five days, half of what he said he needed.

What I saw with my highly inexperienced eyes, was a wonderful job. As I was getting ready to leave his studio after the final sitting, he asked for Mom's address. This I gave him and then asked how much I owed him for the painting. He avoided the question and asked me if I would allow him to enter the painting in an art exhibition coming up the next month. I said sure thing and again asked what I owed. He responded saying he still had a lot of work to do to finish the portrait and once it was completed, he would let me know. In my mind, I thought the price would be around fifty pounds and if I gave him a hundred, he would be happy. I decided to wait until he contacted me. This of course would never take place.

We returned to Little Staughton at the end of our leave and on August 10, we were again on the Battle Order.

The target was the Dijon Marshalling yards and our crew would be one of the illuminators. We took off at 2120 hours.

At 0015 hours from our assigned altitude of twelve thousand feet, we commenced our target run. The weather over the target was clear with a slight haze and visibility considered fair. At 0017 hours from an altitude of twelve thousand feet, we dropped our bomb load, which consisted of twenty-four yellow-headed flares & seven one thousand pound General Purpose bombs. As planned, several loads of flares were dropped before ours. At 0017, the Master Bomber ordered the attacking force to bomb the red and green TI's, which were the last instructions we heard from the Master Bomber. We headed for home and landed at 0255 hours.

Now only two more operations and we would be part of the three or four percent who survived two tours.

Al's mother Mae and his great grandmother Margaretha

Al and his Grandpa Fred Barker

Al, his dad Frank, brothers Jack and Fred and sister Louise

Class at 12 SFTS

Tiger Moths

Fairey Battle

Al with his wings after graduation

Montreal 1942 just prior to sailing on the Queen Elizabeth. right to left
Al Trotter, Charlie James, unknown, Ken Bates, unknown.

Left to right John (Corny) Broad, Al holding puppy mascot, Archie
(Kenneth) Archibald

The crew of F for Freddy Left to Right F/S Bernard Pullin, F/S Kenneth Archibald, F/L Elmer (Al) Trotter, F/S John Rawcliffe, F/S Walter Parfitt, F/S John Thomas Broad – Missing S/L Barcroft (Bart) Mathers

582 Squadron

The White Horse Pub at Little Staughton

Archie (Kenneth Archibald)

The Painting

Bernie Pullin taken August 44

Dr. Ernst Waldschmidt, Bomber Crew Interrogator at the Dulag Luft.

Red Gordon and his sister Grace (courtesy of Don Elliott)

Pilot Officer Don Elliott (Pappy to the Kriegies)(Courtesy of Don Elliott)

Al, Prisoner of War Mug Shot

The circuit at Stalag Luft III (Courtesy Marilyn Walton)

The March (Courtesy USAFA McDermott Library)

Prisoners resting on the March (Courtesy of USAFA McDermott Library)

The 40 Boxcars at Spremburg (Courtesy USAFA McDermott Library)

BBC Radio Monitory (Courtesy of Harold Kious)

Memorial to the Fifty Executed Prisoners (Courtesy Marilyn Walton)

Al and Val on their wedding day, September 1, 1950

Al and Val 2009

CHAPTER ELEVEN
THE LAST SORTIE

It was common practice amongst the crews on a squadron, to allocate some or perhaps even most of their personal belongings, to buddies who had expressed a desire for same in the event, you did not return from a sortie. An example would be "Gee Al, I sure like those boots, may I have them if you get the chop?" "Okay Bill, they are yours." I ended up with the high RAF flying boots and fighter pilot's leather jacket I wore on most trips through this process.

The morning after we failed to return, the boys entitled as per usual practice went to my room to collect their gifts. In this case, they would have been rightly pissed off, as I learned after repatriation, that when they arrived to collect their promised goodies, my Bat Girl had locked my door and refused to give them anything. She had carefully itemized all my personal gear, including a ten-pound note and a fifty-pound cheque, which I had left on my dresser. She packed every thing in crates, and made sure the appropriate base stores personnel picked them up.

My Bat Girl was a cute little English lass who kept Sammy Little's and my uniforms, shoes and rooms in first class condition at all times. She also was so into her job that she would come in very early in the morning whenever Sammy or I were on the Battle order from the night before, just to see if we had survived as well as bring us a hot cup of tea. That is why she refused to let the guys enter my room to collect the items I had promised them, if I went for a chop.

On August 12, 1944, we once again were on the battle order. This time the target was the Opel car factory in Russelsheim. The factory, had once been used to manufacture Opel cars, but was now being used for the manufacture of the fuselage and wings, for flying bombs such as the V1 and V2, which were currently blitzing London and surrounding areas.

This would be our forty- fourth operation, and my thirty- ninth as a Pathfinder. We were to be the blind illuminator, which meant we were one of the first to go in to drop parachutes with attached high performance flares to illuminate the target. The term blind meant there would be cloud cover making it difficult to spot the target visually.

Three hundred and one aircraft were to make up the bomber force for this raid, comprising of ninety-one pathfinders and two hundred and ten in the main force. 582 Squadron provided sixteen Lancasters, which included the Master Bomber and his deputy. In addition six mosquitoes from 109 Squadron also stationed at Little Staughton, joined us as route-markers. We were to commence bombing the target area at 0015 hours. The following is the summary of events taken from the 582 Squadron Operational Record Books.

The weather over the target area was 2-5/10 cloud. Tops 14,000 feet. Flares were dropped at the appointed hour but were somewhat scattered and gave indifferent illumination owing to haze. When the Master Bomber arrived over the target, there was a good concentration of Green TIs. These were followed by salvos of mixed reds and greens, which fell in the middle of the greens. Visual identification being impossible, orders were given to bomb the centre of these mixed salvos. Several loads of incendiaries dropped in scattered fashion before H hour did not improve chances of visual identification. Fires covered an area of 1 1/2 miles around the TIs and instructions were given to bomb the centre of fires. The general impression is that the attack began somewhat haphazardly, but pulled together in the later stages. Defences – Moderate-high flak barrage at 18-19,000 feet. Much fighter activity en route out and home. 1 was damaged by flak.

We took off at 2205 hours. At approximately 0010 – 0017 hours, we attacked the target and headed for home.

Around 01:30 hours, GMT, while on the return trip, all hell broke loose when an undetected night fighter suddenly attacked us from below. We were approximately one hundred and ninety five miles or one hour from Dunkirk on the French Coast. There were numerous explosions and both starboard engines were on fire. There was little or no feel on my control column, and although the aileron controls seemed capable of keeping the aircraft laterally, more or less level, the elevator and rudder controls were completely non-responsive. The aircraft seemed to be in a series of stalls and subsequent recoveries. It was apparent that our only possibility of survival was to abandon the aircraft.

I gave the order immediately, which was followed by John, the engineer, and Bart, the navigator quickly proceeding to the forward escape hatch. I remember Bart squeezing my shoulder as he hurried past. As Bernie was already down in the nose position, it was reasonable to assume he would have opened the escape hatch, and would have been the first to leave the aircraft.

The aircraft was now gyrating wildly, almost completely out of control, and it was becoming obvious that I should be leaving this burning mass; however, I had not heard or seen anything of my Gunners. I looked back at what was left of the now burning fuselage, and it appeared Corny the wireless operator was dead or severely wounded. Because of smoke and other wreckage, neither, Walter or Archie's (the Gunners) positions were identifiable.

My reaction of not leaving immediately was stupid, because there was absolutely nothing else I could do under the circumstances, but I still found it extremely difficult to abandon the rest of my crew.

Although it was likely only seconds since I unbuckled my seat belt, I found that because of the severe positive and negative G factors, I was bouncing around like a tennis ball. For what seemed like an eternity, I struggled and finally reached the forward escape hatch. As I tried to get out the hatch, I spotted Bernie, still sitting up forward. To this day, I have no idea why he had not bailed out, and can only speculate as to the reason. Knowing Bernie and his undying loyalty to me, I think it possible he was not about to leave the aircraft until he knew I was safely out. Once free of the aircraft, I tried to reach the D ring to deploy my parachute. For milli seconds I could not find it and I panicked, actually clawing through some of the leather on my flying jacket, thinking that I had forgotten to secure the parachute leg straps prior to reaching the enemy coast.

Some smaller pilots wore seat pack parachutes that were very uncomfortable when fully buckled up, and so some of us would not fully buckle them up until we approached the enemy coastline. The rest of the crew wore snap on chest packs.

I finally found the D ring and immediately pulled it. The sudden opening jolt plus the billowing noise of the deploying chute was certainly the most wonderful feeling and sound I have ever experienced.

After the chute opened, I think I had one full oscillation. I really do not know how many, as its relative importance at the time had really little or no significance. The next wonderful incident was the sudden stop as I landed in the trees on the side of a mountain.

After the war, I dropped hundreds of Army paratroopers and when I explained my experience the night our aircraft had been shot down the consensus from the experts, was that I must have baled out at a very low altitude, perhaps as low as five hundred feet above the ground. In any event, I must have been in "F" for Freddy for several thousand feet of free fall and certainly, my survival would appear to have been in the hands of the "powers that be."

After landing (so to speak), I realized that I was hanging in a tree on what appeared to be a fairly high mountain. My chute was holding me off the ground because it had spread over an area of spindly sapling trees. When I tried to pull myself up the trees, the small branches would not support me. To compound the problem, it was apparent that well below me was a river (I learned later it was likely the Moselle) and in the darkness it appeared that if I released my parachute harness, I could fall into the river below.

While I paused to assess the situation and my options, if any, I could hear the bombers passing overhead on their way back to England. To say I felt sorry for myself would be the under statement of the century. I felt very alone.

Now another problem came to the forefront. My mother was not medically well and I realized that when the government advised my parents that I was missing, the result could be fatal for her. Even though I did not believe in mental telepathy, I kept repeating, "I'm okay mother, I'm okay."

After the war, when I returned home, my father said at the exact time (taking into consideration the different time zones) when I was trying to mentally communicate with mother, she was resting on her chesterfield, and she woke up screaming "something has happened to Elmer!" over and over again. Despite dad's attempt to assure her that she had experienced a nightmare, she would not believe dad was right. To this day, I still believe this was more than coincidence and my concentration on her may have contributed to getting the message through.

Getting back to my immediate problem, I decided that I could not hang there all night. I took a firm grip with my left hand on several of the limbs and struck the parachute release mechanism with my right hand. Although I anticipated a long drop, I only fell approximately six inches. My poor old back sure ached for a long time afterwards, and if you have ever inadvertently stepped off a sidewalk, you will have some idea of what I experienced. Now however, I had to "get my act together" and make sensible plans immediately if I were to have any hope of a successful evasion.

CHAPTER TWELVE
EVASION AND CAPTURE

I was lucky in that I had not lost my escape kit as many others had when baling out of the aircraft. The kit contained such items as a small folded map of the area we would be flying over on any particular sortie. It also contained a compass, a plastic bag for water, barley sugar candies, horlicks tablets, to keep you alert and a small knife. Unlike the American flyers, we did not carry revolvers. The theory was what good would it do you? If you happened across German soldiers, pulling the weapon out could only result in being shot.

After giving my current predicament some considerable thought I decided that I would climb up the hillside rather than down, deeming it the safest procedure. Now I could hear dogs barking above me, and assumed that might indicate the presence of a military lookout or maybe a search party, so I decided to maintain a constant, more or less level track and skirt around the suspected enemy.

In a situation, such as my current one, in enemy territory and in the dark, your imagination tends to take charge, and I feel over kill becomes a real factor, reflecting negatively on your ability to evacuate the crash site area quickly.

After approximately one hour of carefully avoiding enemy troops, who in every case turned out to be only trees, I entered a vineyard. I decided to proceed downhill now as I was in an area that was obviously under human maintenance. This would allow me to proceed more quickly towards the river and possibly better terrain for evading.

When I reached the bottom of the vineyard, which took about thirty minutes, I discovered a paved road between the river, and myself, however, to my chagrin, I could also hear human voices and laughing a short distance away, and assumed it could be a military checkpoint. The river appeared to be a large stream, only twenty-five or thirty yards across. With dawn not far away, and with what appeared to be a heavily wooded area on the other side, I decided it would be in my best interest to get to the other side of the river as soon as possible.

Having made up my mind, I removed my leather-flying jacket and slowly entered the stream, which initially appeared only waist deep with very little current. That made me very happy, because my swimming ability could be at the best, described as dog paddle only. It took about fifteen or twenty minutes to cross the "mighty" river, and I only had to resort to dog paddling for maybe four or five minutes. Once on the other side, it was only a few yards to the woods, which were dense. For evasion purposes, they obviously provided excellent cover and as I soon realized, relatively easy walking. I now took out my compass and set course due west, hopefully toward Allied forces. I still had not pinpointed my position on my escape map, but I felt I would have time to do so when I found a good area to hibernate temporarily for the rest of the day light hours.

I guess I walked for approximately thirty or forty minutes. Daybreak was rapidly approaching, so I found a nice bush under which I settled down to spend the daylight hours, in accordance with the accepted rules for evasion, and hopefully, to get some much-needed rest after the ordeal I had just been through.

In due course, I did fall asleep for a couple of hours. When I woke up, I was amazed at the peaceful surroundings. There were no human associated noises of any kind, only birds singing and squirrels chirping as they were running up and down the trees, almost as if Mother Nature was putting on a show especially for me. After another couple of hours with nothing but nature's calm, and after having established my approximate position on my map and I do mean approximate, I finally decided that as long as I stayed in a forest environment, I would be able to make good time with little risk of apprehension. The theory sounded reasonable.

I put on my socks and flying boots, which had dried in the few hours I had them off, and with my flying jacket over my shoulder, I set off on a compass heading of two hundred and eighty degrees. I hoped I was more or less heading towards the Duchy of Luxembourg, which was notorious for its loyalty flip- flopping, dependant on which of the major powers was winning. In that we were advancing on all fronts, I could assume they were our Allies now.

Trying to be very vigilant, I set off westbound, stopping regularly to listen for any sounds that I could consider threatening to my evasion. I made good time with no evidence whatsoever of any human habitation; however, things were about to change.

As I approached an opening in the forest, I slowed to a virtual stop to check out a small meadow for other human beings, before breaking my cover. The meadow seemed to be devoid of any inhabitants other than myself, so after a few more minutes of studying the area, I ventured out into the meadow. Suddenly, from my right, appeared two uniformed and armed soldiers. Both, I found out later were members of the German equivalent to the British Home Guard. They had been resting just in the shade of the forest at the edge of the meadow. One of them had a rifle and the other had a double-barrelled shotgun. The latter appeared to be intoxicated and his actions left no doubt in my mind that he wanted to use me as a target. Happily, for me, every time he raised his shotgun towards me, his comrade would push the gun down and seemingly reprimand him. After searching me for weapons, we headed off to their village (*post war research indicated that it was likely the village of Papiermuhle, just east of Drohn-Neumagan*) which seemed to be approximately four to five miles east of where they captured me.

When we reached the village, the locals quickly gathered to see this "enemy" of the Reich. I felt like a monkey in the zoo with them coming up to me, feeling my flight jacket, flying boots, and speaking to me in a language I did not understand. At no time did I sense any hostility, only curiosity.

I offered a couple of the youngsters some of my high energy escape candies but the man who was doing all the talking quickly took it away from them. He handed one of them to me and pointed to my mouth. This I took as meaning "you eat first" which I did and after a few minutes, when he was satisfied the candy was not poison, he gave the rest back to the kids, smiled at me, said "danke", and offered me a glass of water, which was much appreciated.

Shortly after I finished drinking the water, two new soldiers took over and took me to the city of Trier, which I thought was the capital of Luxembourg. The walk took about three hours, primarily because they appeared to be much older than I was, and took several smoke breaks on the way down. Each time they stopped and lit up a cigarette, they always gave me one as well, mind you the cigarettes we were smoking up until a few hours ago, belonged to me. After we reached the jail in what I assumed was Trier, they bid me good-bye, shook my hand, and my new jailers quickly lodged me in a cell, no bed but a pile of hay, on which I flopped and soon fell asleep.

Some time later I awoke with the arrival of another "guest of Deutschland" coming into my cell. Although we recognized one another, we did not acknowledge same for some time, and then only by way of a handshake and some whispering. It was my Australian navigator, Bart Mathers. We had been trained that in the event of capture, we were not to indicate any recognition of another airman as the interrogators would undoubtedly play us off one against the other.

The next morning, the guards took us up to the local, what we believed to be Gestapo Headquarters. We were ushered into an office and shortly there after, an officer in a black uniform, complete with a black swastika on a blood red armband on his upper left arm, and wearing jackboots entered the office. He stopped in front of us, clicked his boots to attention, and gave the Nazi salute. We responded with our normal salute. He then repeated "Nein, nein!" and again gave the Nazi salute. Recognizing the nein meant no; I said "nein, nein" to him. His reaction was a spontaneous punch to my face.

Having had boxing as a hobby for many years, I recognized a telegraphed punch, and went with it, so a split lip and a bruised youthful ego was the only damage I suffered. My natural Irish reaction was to respond, but Bart grabbed a handful of my hair and hauled me backwards, which likely saved my life. In retrospect, it was obvious that my actions in that incident were to say the least, nothing but youthful stupidity, the result of which could have been fatal but for Bart's intervention.

The remainder of the interrogation involved basic questions such as, where were you based? What type of aircraft were you flying? What was your target? To which we simply responded with our name, rank and service number, as required by the Geneva Convention.

The officer's demeanour appeared to be one of sheer boredom to say the least, and perhaps thankfully so from our point of view. When guards took us from his office, they separated Bart and me and although we know we were both in Stalag Luft III, we were obviously in different compounds: in any event, we never met again. We came close during the Korean War when he was flying for Quantas and I was flying with the Royal Canadian Air Force. We missed each other by a day on two occasions: once in Tokyo and once in Vancouver.

After our incident with the German officer, they took me to a Luftwaffe base fairly close to Trier, and turned me over to base personnel who treated me with respect, which I found rather overwhelming. In this regard, and in the future of my tenure as a prisoner, I discovered, in many cases it was the norm for our captured airmen to be reasonably well treated by the Luftwaffe. It was sort of an Esprit de Corp. In any event, there were many stories re-told in the camp at Stalag Luft III, of airmen, who after successfully parachuting from doomed aircraft, had been captured by ground troops known as the Wehrmacht oft times threatened with almost certain execution by their captors and being rescued by Luftwaffe personnel arriving in the so-called "nick of time."

It was here I received my first real meal since leaving Little Staughton. After dinner, the air raid sirens sounded and the guards responsible for my security took me to the air raid shelter with hundreds of other Luftwaffe and civilian support personnel.

Shortly after arriving at the shelter, a young lad about twelve or thirteen years old approached me, and addressed me in very good English. He stated there were two Luftwaffe aircrew officers that believed they were the crew who had shot me down, and they wanted to meet me. I agreed. Did I have a choice? They approached me and stated in German (translated into English by the young man) that they were the crew of a (Junkers) JU88 who had shot down a Lancaster bomber two nights before and they believed it was my aircraft. I said; "That was not a nice thing to do," to which they laughed and replied, "Better we shoot you down than you shoot us down."

Following this rather interesting meeting, which resolved nothing; my escorts took me over to the shelter entrance and pointed upward where a great number of USAF bombers were engaged in a very noisy battle with what appeared to be Luftwaffe Messerschmitt 109s and Fochewulf 190s. Suddenly as we watched the battle above, an aircraft was shot down. Enveloped in a huge plume of smoke and fire, it was impossible to identify whether it was friend or foe. The young interpreter said people wanted to know was it a USAF bomber to which I replied, "No, it's an ME109. My guess was as good as theirs was, and reflected what I hoped was true...

CHAPTER THIRTEEN
THE INTERROGATION

Later in the day, in the custody of three guards, I, along with other prisoners, boarded a train to Frankfurt am Main, en route to the infamous prisoner interrogation centre, better known as Dulag Luft. Until the authorities at Dulag Luft decided to send you to a permanent Prisoner of War camp, they informed no one, including the International Red Cross, you were a POW. In other words, you were still officially MIA (missing in action).

I cannot remember how many hours it took to reach Frankfurt am Main, but it was certainly most of the night. When we arrived at the Frankfurt railway station, I was amazed at the damage inflicted by our raids. The station roof was predominately constructed of heavy-duty paned glass, the majority of which was shattered beyond repair by Allied bombing. While waiting for transport to take us the approximate twelve or so miles to Dulag Luft at Wetzlar, a male adult kept walking around our little group, staring at me with wild eyes. He suddenly pushed by the guards and spat in my face. Strange as it may seem, I was not angry. As I wiped the spittle off my face, I reconciled my lack of anger by assuming, because of one of our raids, he may have lost some or perhaps all of his loved ones. Under similar circumstances, with the shoe on the other foot, what would my reaction have been? Was I being philosophical? Perhaps.

Shortly thereafter, our transport arrived and our thirteen-mile trip to Oberursel/Wetzlar was soon over. I must admit this was the first time I began to experience grave concern for what the future might have in store for me.

On the night before we took off on this mission, Archie, Bernie and I, engaged in some horseplay, and during the scuffling, one of them grabbed and accidentally broke the neck chain holding my service identification (dog tags). Unfortunately, I just tossed them up on my dresser with the intention of having them fixed the next day. However, the next morning we were once again on the Battle Order. With all the items requiring my attention prior to take-off such as, air test of our aircraft prior to its being bombed up, general and specialized briefings involving, navigation, meteorology, careless or otherwise, on my part, they did not get fixed. Now here I was a prisoner, about to face interrogation by the enemy, with no military identification. The situation was anything but in my favour.

The guards quickly took me to a cell, approximately five feet by eight feet. It had one opaque window, heavy-duty bars, and what, was best be described, as an excuse for a bed. The first thing I noted was that the cell was stifling hot, and obviously, I had no control over that feature in any way. It was the middle of August, with normal temperatures in the eighties (Fahrenheit). They certainly were not doing this in my best interest. Some time later, the guards arrived and with little or no formality, took me for my first interrogation.

I was ushered into a large office where a uniformed German officer, who introduced himself as Hauptman Dr.Waldschmidt, greeted me. Through research, I learned he was Major Waldschmidt, the top interrogator in the Bomber Section, and a former Professor of Indiology at Gottingen University. In any event, his spoken English was very fluent.

He offered me a cigarette, which I gratefully accepted as the guards had confiscated mine when I first was captured. The session was of short duration because I answered every question regardless of its content, with "my name is Trotter, my rank is Flight Lieutenant, and my serial number is J19643." This response was in accordance with the Geneva Convention and as directed by our own intelligence officers.

I obviously was trying Dr. Waldschmidt's patience, and although he had no doubt heard similar responses to mine many times, he had one little difference in my case, namely I had no Military ID. He took the moment of my departure from his office to remind me that I had no identification, and as such left myself open to suspicion as to my real identity.

After my return to my cell, I pondered my predicament with no significant or appropriate course of action, for the next session with Dr. Waldschmidt. My God was it ever hot in my cell! The only hope I had of getting any sleep was to get rid of my clothes and to keep as still as possible.

The next morning, a guard brought me a pitcher of lukewarm water, which I truly appreciated because I was very dehydrated from the intense heat, which obviously resulted in heavy duty sweating.

My second day of interrogation went much the same as the first. I had a cigarette, the Dr. lost his temper, and I went back to my cell. Shortly after returning this time, a guard arrived with some barley soup and a slice of black bread. I could hardly find any barley in the soup, and the bread was heavy, black and without any oleo or butter. I can only describe it as an appetite spoiler. I greedily ate both items, although under normal circumstances, they would be inedible. However, when you have had only one meal in two days you will eat most anything and enjoy it while doing so.

Getting back to my own circumstances, I decided that I would try new tactics on Dr. Waldschmidt, realizing of course this was normally considered a no-no according to directions from our Intelligence Officers.

I decided the current dilemma, in which I found myself, gave them some degree of legality to execute me as a spy. If I could not legally identify myself, as long as I did not "spill my guts" with regard to any aspect of our military operations, anything was worth a try.

Day three and four were not unlike the previous ones, except I took note of the numerous large black and white photographs that circled the Doctor's office. It appeared the vast majority had been taken in what I thought were African countries.

The one big difference in his questioning on days three and four was his disclosure of items about my past. Facts such as, my having attended Central Collegiate in Moose Jaw Saskatchewan, of my grandfather being a CPR Locomotive Engineer and my father's relatives living in Madoc, Ontario. There was other information about Dad, of which I had no knowledge but I found out after the war, were true. Waldschmidt also knew 582 Squadron had recently acquired a new Commanding Officer. Although I was somewhat surprised, I tried to be nonchalant; once again, our Intelligence had advised us not to sell the Luftwaffe Interrogators short, as they were truly experts at their trade.

When back at my cell I gave the days occurrences some thoughts; where did they got all their information about me? The only common denominator was the media. In Canada when you graduated from pilot training, the local media cite almost your whole life history complete with your photo. I suspect the same applied in our Allies homelands.

There was no doubt, I was becoming depressed with the lack of food, intense heat, and observation of the numerous scratches on the wall, previous occupants had used to keep track of their "vacation at the beautiful destination resort of Dulag Luft", some of which went on for weeks.

Day five went quite well I thought. After he asked me to be seated and allowed me my normal one a day cigarette, I quickly asked him questions about his very interesting pictures. I was amazed at how he obviously enjoyed describing in detail, the demography of the various places depicted in the photographs. I also realized that his pre-war vocation must have been in the scientific field of some sort, as the photos and comments were all applicable to "have not" countries.

While I was asking questions and he was providing lengthy answers, I was rapidly smoking my cigarette. When I was stubbing out the last few millimetres, I would say, "did I ever enjoy that cigarette," and he would allow me to have another one. I must say that at no time did I believe that I was outsmarting him, and he may well have realized what I was up to, but it was obvious he thoroughly enjoyed the opportunity to talk about the "love of his life." In any event, he would eventually get back to the purpose of why I was in his office, and although his shouting tirades were definitely moderating, the result was always the same, back to my luxurious suite and real life.

Days six and seven were pretty much the same as day five, although there was more time spent with him asking questions and me giving the same answers; name, rank and serial number. The one item he brought up more and more often was it was my responsibility to prove to their satisfaction, that I was just an allied flyer. Name rank and serial number was my answer.

Day eight started with an earlier than normal appearance before Dr. Waldschmidt. His opening remarks advised me that the Commandant had lost his patience with me, because he felt I was making no effort to prove I was not an enemy agent. "Therefore, I ask you for the last time, will you answer these very simple questions?" I replied; "my name is Trotter, my rank is Flight Lieutenant and my number is J19643.

His violent reaction of pounding his desk and shouting what I assumed were obscenities was surprising, to say the least. Could this be the same "gentleman," who on earlier sessions, calmly and with obvious heartfelt feelings, spoke of Africa and Asia and its starving millions? Now he was fiercely screaming; "you will be executed tomorrow morning as a spy!"

The guards arrived as if on cue, and ushered me back to my cell. It was a very long night and I can assure you I did not sleep one wink. My mind was full of questions: are they serious? If they really mean to execute me, how would they do it? What would my parents be told if anything? Am I mentally strong enough to withhold emotion?

I think it is important for my readers to understand, that I sincerely believe the preceding week had emotionally strengthened, rather than weakened my resolve. I had likely lost most of my family (crew), I could not but help be emotionally affected by the heat treatment, lack of food and water, the seemingly endless questions, knowing that my inability to produce my "dog tags" constituted a dicey situation, and finally realizing that nobody, but nobody knew that I was alive. Bart knew I survived, but where was Bart now?

It is strange how the human mind operates under duress. In my own situation, I strongly believe that the most positive mental reaction occurred on about the fifth or sixth day following my incarceration in Dulag Luft. The actual situation developed at night when I was mentally cataloguing the items pertinent to my incarceration. My final analysis was "shoot me, get it over with!" In any event, I became very positive about any future interaction with my captors. I firmly believed that they did not have one chance in hell of me betraying my crew, my parents, my squadron mates, the RCAF, or my Country, so they might as well get on with whatever they had in mind to do.

I am certainly not suggesting it was bravado, but more an acceptance of reality, after all, they held all the aces, and in my mind, only they knew what the final solution would be.

At approximately 05:00 hours, an officer, and two guards arrived at my cell. I am not too sure of the scenario that followed; I felt it was all a dream. Maybe I was in a partial coma; in any event, I am not certain of the precise sequence of events.

They took me out of the building into a small yard and tied my hands behind me around a post. A small group of seven or eight soldiers was a few yards in front of me. The officer tied a blindfold over my eyes; I do not recall the officer saying anything to me like the Hollywood scenario, last cigarette or anything to say?

All I kept telling myself was "they're not serious; this is just part of the game." When the Officer shouted commands in German, I obviously did not understand what he was saying, however when I heard the bolts of the rifles ramming bullets into the chambers, that was a language I did understand, My last thought was "will the bullets burn"?

When the Officer gave what I thought to be the command to fire, followed immediately by him grasping my shoulder, I thought I was dead. He then took the blindfold off, and stated that the Commandant had given me another chance because I was so young. I was twenty-one. Then they took me up to Dr. Waldschmidt's office, and en route I suddenly realized that the scenario currently unfolding was not unlike what our Intelligence Officers had said could occur. I obviously looked for something positive in my favour and suddenly experienced some false bravado.

After a short address in which the Doctor reiterated what the Firing Squad Officer in charge had said about my youth, and my opportunity for a second chance. He again gave me the questionnaire for completion. With my new positive outlook based on the most recent sequence of events, and the positive encouragement building within, I printed my name, rank, and serial number on the paper and drew a big X through the three pages of questions. Well the reaction from the Doctor was, as you would expect, ugly to say the least. As the guards took me away, Dr Waldschmidt's final admonishment to me was "you will definitely be executed tomorrow morning."

Once back in my "oven," regardless of my feeling that everything would be okay, there was still a very serious question, what did Dr. Waldschmidt hope to prove? This thought sent me into another sleepless night, particularly when it was obvious that he was not I repeat not, providing me with an opportunity to change my mind.

Despite my growing negative feeling, I did doze off a few times because of sheer fatigue and the excessive high temperature in the cell. In general, a feeling of failure took over my thought process, and when the guards arrived, I believe I had resigned myself to the worst-case scenario, and had made peace with myself and with God. I kept saying to my self without any real enthusiasm, "they are only kidding."

When the guards arrived and again took me from my cell to a repeat of the previous day's exercise, there was one big difference. This time I was internally calm. As I was tied to the post in front of the firing squad, the only thoughts I recalled were, would anyone ever know what happened to me?, will I feel the bullets strike me?, I cannot in retrospect understand why I was so calm or had I temporarily lapsed into a partial coma? In any event, after what seemed to be an eternity, the Firing Squad Commander untied me. He said absolutely nothing, and when I was taken back to Dr. Waldschmidt's office, even he made no mention of the morning's events. He offered and I accepted a cigarette. He then abruptly asked if I had any requests with which he might be able to help me.

I was rather astounded after what had taken place over the past forty eight hours, how-ever, I quickly recalled what our Intelligence Officers had often appraised us of at our regular briefings, how on some occasions, the interrogators would try to get your trust by being the nice guy. In any case I replied, "Yes, turn off the bloody heat and open the window to allow fresh air to enter." He wrote something down on a pad and then asked "anything else"? Therefore, I gave him a list, which included some food and drinking water, a shower and the opportunity to shave, a book to read, and most importantly a ticket back to Canada.

The Doctor stood up, held out his hand, and said, "Good luck, I'm afraid I can't give you a ticket home, but you will be sent to a permanent POW camp within the next forty-eight hours." He then saluted, and the guards took me back to my cell.

I sat down on my bed, at which time I became very emotional, I think I took turns laughing and crying intermittently, after all, in the last sixty minutes I had gone from almost certain death to almost certain in comparison, freedom. All I could say repeatedly was "thank you God."

Within an hour, the heat was off, a guard opened my window, and another guard brought me a cheese sandwich. It tasted like Canadian cheddar; however, the bread was the German black variety without oleomargarine, but it mattered not, it tasted like a gourmet sandwich to me. The guard took me to a washroom where there was only cold water, a well used bar of German lather-less hand soap, and a worn out double bladed razor. The shave was agonizing to say the least, but under the circumstances, it was refreshing.

The next day I left for Stalag Luft III at Sagan in Poland. It was like a breath of fresh air; no, it was much better than that, maybe it was almost like being reborn, I WAS ALIVE!

CHAPTER FOURTEEN
ARRIVAL AT STALAG LUFT III

As I walked through the gate at Stalag Luft III, I felt like I was almost free, and now I had been given a reasonable chance of survival. There was absolutely no doubt my emotions were at an all time high. I was suddenly amongst friends as opposed to the three days previous, when I was facing what appeared to be certain death at the hands of a firing squad. In any event, there was no way I could stop the tears of happiness from flowing down my face, which in turn made it impossible to recognize those surrounding me. I was not embarrassed in any way for my crying like a baby. However, one thing was almost immediately apparent. I could not recognize any of those surrounding me, and obviously the same problem applied to their recognition of me.

The scepticisms associated with the identification of new arrivals, was fully justified. It was apparently not uncommon for our captors to plant one of their own amongst incoming new arrivals. However, as I soon discovered, our own POW security system was very efficient in their interrogation of new arrivals, there-by ensuring they were in fact bona fide Allied prisoners. Once again, for several days my lack of identification tags would haunt me, as the Prisoner's Security system threw hundreds of questions at me, not stopping until they satisfied themselves, that I was who I claimed to be. I was then assigned to a room in one of the barracks, which was predominately occupied by Canadians. I was in the East Compound in Hut A, room 12.

During the research and writing of this book, I spoke with Don Elliott, known as "Pappy" to the Kriegies. He said he was housed in room 13 just across the hall from me, and was interested in speaking with me in that I was from Tuberose Saskatchewan, not far from his home town of Swift Current.

CHAPTER FIFTEEN
DON ELLIOTTS STORY

Don had enlisted with the RCAF June 15, 1940 and after completion of his training, commissioned as a Pilot Officer. He served with 99 RAF Squadron, flying in Wellington 1Cs. Don was an observer and when flying combat missions, would navigate the aircraft to the city to be bombed. He would then go to the nose of the aircraft, guide the pilot to the designated target and then release the bombs.

In the early morning hours of July 8, 1941, while running up on the railway station in Cologne, Don's aircraft was coned by searchlights at about fifteen thousand feet and the aircraft severely hit by flak. The pilot, Pilot Officer Masters immediately ordered the crew to bail out. All crewmembers survived and having landed by a flak battery, they were picked up almost immediately. The following is Don's recollection of bailing out.

"It was a long journey back to the navigator's table, about 15 feet to get my parachute and then return to the front of the aircraft in order to jump out of the hatch in the nose.

Once I tore off my oxygen and intercom tubes and released my foot from a flying boot that flak splinters had jammed under the bottom step of the three which lead down from the cabin, all went well. After briefly considering the alternative, about one millisecond, I did not hesitate to jump. When I left the aircraft, I was clutching the rip cord of the parachute, which when pulled would open it. I now believe I neglected to do so.

One's terminal velocity in these circumstances reaches 120 miles per hour so I had about a minute and a half to think about my situation. My first thought was that there would be a flash of light and then I would be dead. My next thought was that I should get in touch with my mother at Swift Current Saskatchewan, by ESP and tell her I was in a bit of trouble. As soon as I finished that, I must have pulled the ripcord because my parachute opened. I believe I was then up about 1,000 feet. There was a full moon and I could see the horizon and the ground clearly. The landing was a "piece of cake".

As soon as I took off my parachute harness, I felt I should get in touch with my mother once more and cancel my original message. I went into ESP mode again and informed her that I was now safe and sound.

Four years later when I came home to Swift Current, my first question to my mother was whether or not she had received my message. I was more than a little disappointed when she said she had not! Obviously ESP does not always work when you want it to."

After capture and interrogation at the Dulag Luft in Frankfurt, Don was sent to Oflag VIIC in Laufen until August 1941. From there it was to OflagXC Lubeck to November '41, Oflag VIB- Warberg to April'42, Oflag XXIB Schrubin, Poland to April '43 Stalag Luft III – Sagan to January'45.

Just before the Death March, Don developed strep throat and was transferred to the hospital at Stalag VIIIC- Sagan where he remained until released by Russian Troops, February 16, 1945.

He walked for seven days to Oels, now in Poland and then travelled by boxcar for fourteen days and over 600 miles to Odessa on the Black Sea. From there he travelled on the Duchess of Bedford to Liverpool, arriving April 12, 1945.

In 1947, Don married Grace Gordon, Red Gordon's sister. They have three children, Gordon, Peter and Barbara and spend their time raising Holstein heifers at Blue Heaven Farm, in Cheltenham Ontario.

Perhaps it was Pappy, who helped me pass the identity test.

CHAPTER SIXTEEN
PRISON LIFE IN GENERAL

My first night in my new bunk, the pallias (mattress of straw) apparently held more bedbugs than straw, and they proceeded to eat me alive. To resolve the problem, I slept on a bench for the first five days, as one of the old-timers provided a bed bug killer, a procedure, which was necessary on a regular basis. I was extremely allergic to bed bug bites and to this day, even the mention of them causes me to start scratching. The old timers had a game of hunting the bed bugs with torches to see who could find and kill the most. I think someone achieved a count of over one hundred in one night. As I recall the hunt required the use of a home made torch, I think the fire hazard would have been rated as extreme.

There were incidents of experienced pilots, newly arrived at the camp, to suffer from nightmares for a period of time. In the middle of the night, they would scream out "Abandon aircraft, abandon aircraft!" This resulted in many POWs baling out of their bunks, and landing in a heap on the floor.

Another incident involving new arrivals, is worthy of mention. New arrivals would usually get the top bunks in their assigned room, and after every one had retired and were asleep or almost there, all of a sudden a newly arrived sprog would drop a boot to the floor with a loud thud, waking up all those at or on the verge of sleeping. We would wait and wait and finally someone would yell, "Will you drop the other damn boot so we can get some rest!" What had happened was the sprog had dropped his first boot, and then fell asleep from shear exhaustion before even getting the other boot off.

We spent our days playing bridge, lots of bridge. I became so proficient at the game, that when I returned home to Canada I was able to beat my Dad and his cohorts, who were considered masters of the game.

Physical fitness was considered an absolute must because of the mystery surrounding our future. We also had homemade hobbyhorses that were very popular exercise vehicles, even while being used for dispensing sand from escape tunnel excavations. Our most common exercise consisted of walking the perimeter of the camp every day maybe four or five times, I am not certain, but I think one circuit was a good half mile. In addition, we could occasionally play a little game of soccer and the occasional ball game.

We had a Canadian ex Philadelphia Athletics pitcher whose name was Phil Marchildon. In any event having been a baseball pitcher myself, but certainly not anywhere near Phil's ability, I agreed to catch for him while he put on a demonstration for the residents of our camp. My sanity certainly could be questioned. My mitt as I recall, either was made by the residents or was softball quality. Phil was known for his fastball and after ten or fifteen minutes, my poor old hand could attest to the honesty of his claim. We put on this show several times, but with the onset of cold weather, I with Phil's agreement called a halt to the punishment I was taking. Phil promised me if he made it back to the major leagues after the war, he would gladly provide my friends and I with first class seats for the game or games. I must admit I never followed up on his offer, however I do know he did make it back to the major leagues and in 1946 became the number one pitcher for the Philadelphia Athletics.

I think most if not all Kregies would agree, that boredom next to hunger was the most common malady suffered by POW's. The boredom without doubt meant lots of time to think, and I mean, LOTS of TIME to THINK. I do not believe I ever stopped wondering what had become of my crew. I knew Bart was alive, but where was he? Had John survived the baling out? What about Archie, Bernie, John and Corny? Had any of them successfully abandoned the burning aircraft? If not, had their bodies been found? Did someone bury them? Had Bernie been waiting for me to go before he followed? There were so many unanswered questions.

I found out after the war that both Bart and John had been prisoners, in Stalag Luft III but in different compounds. John being a non commissioned officer (NCO) would be in a different compound again, yet our paths never crossed.

We were allowed to write one mini letter each month, consisting of the equivalent of one page. Receiving letters was almost as important to us as the Red Cross parcels containing food and other things.

At this stage of the war, with the massive destruction of Germany's railway network, and other components of her transportation systems by the Allied Air Forces, we were lucky, if we received even one Red Cross parcel per month, and letters from home were often received even more infrequently.

The Canadian Red Cross parcels were currently in short supply, but when they got through, excellent, not only for our consumption, but as a guard bargaining tool. I believe the average parcel contained

6 ounces chocolate
1 small can of jam
1ounce salt and pepper
12 biscuits
6 ounces prunes
12 ounces bully beef
10 ounces of ham
7 ounces raisins
4 ounces cheese
6 ounces coffee
4 ounces tea
8 ounces salmon
8 ounces powdered milk
1 can sardines
1 bar of soap

For things like socks, scarves and cigarettes we would request them from home, and just hope they would get to us.

CHAPTER SEVENTEEN

WHAT MADE STALAG LUFT III TICK?

Stalag Luft III was unfortunately, the most famous of all German POW camps for its Prisoner Escape history and was made even more so by the movie The Great Escape of Hollywood fame. It recognized the fantastic Engineering accomplishment of building the longest tunnel (three hundred and fifty feet), deepest (thirty feet), and largest number of escapers (seventy three) to initially escape at one time from a POW camp. It unfortunately, is the most infamous because of the fifty re-captured prisoners who were cold-bloodedly murdered by the Gestapo, on Hitler's orders.

It goes without saying, that the fantastic talents displayed, by the prisoners in a myriad of ways with-in the confines of the camp was to say the least, over-whelming. To list only a few, the camp was blessed with expert tradesmen in carpentry, construction engineering, electricians, miners, lithographers, map makers, clothiers, tailors, excavation engineers, teachers, photographers, pharmacists, welders, men of the cloth, professional play directors and writers, linguists etc. When you bear in mind that all of these professionals had only their accumulated knowledge, but little or no tools of their trade with which to practice their careers, it makes their actual accomplishments as escape artists all the more mind-boggling. I think, it was also awe inspiring, to see the generally positive morale evident in the vast majority of the inmates, which included many who had been prisoners in excess of three to four years.

We were always hungry. I remember the time the Commandants little dachshund disappeared. The Commandant had us all lined up in a hollow square with machine gunners in the middle. He threatened to have us shot if someone did not inform him of the dog's whereabouts. No one confessed and no one was shot. I am sure the little dog was eaten, as he was apparently never found.

We also had, rat and bird traps and we were not above eating the odd cat. On one occasion, a big cat brought a rabbit into the compound. He was quickly relieved of his prize and under normal circumstances, would himself be a candidate for the stew pot. On this occasion, a would, be "Philadelphia Lawyer" suggested, that since the cat had brought a rabbit in for the stew pot, he should be given a temporary reprieve in the hope he might bring in another rabbit. I have no idea what the final outcome was, but I must admit, I never saw a cat loose in the camp again, and can only assume his demise was similar to that of the rabbit.

Approximately one month after my arrival at Stalag Luft III, an announcement was made over the Tannoy, the camp public address system. There was a shipment of sauerkraut available at the entrance gate. This apparent and questionable generosity occurred periodically, and although we knew it only resulted because the sauerkraut was too sauer (sic) for the German troops, we were never the less, most grateful. Each room would designate one member of their group, to hurry over to the gate with a large pewter bowl and load up.

To appreciate our situation, one must understand that earlier in the war before the Allies accomplished their successful invasion, the Red Cross provided food parcels on a regular basis. As the Allied Air Forces became more successful in their destruction of the German transportation system, so did, the regularity of food parcels and deliveries become sporadic to say the least. As a result, hunger pangs were a common malady amongst all of us.

When we got our basin of food, if you could call it that, back to our barracks, we proceeded to literally fry the hell out of it, with the purpose ill conceived as the almost immediate future would prove, of killing any germs that might be present as a direct result of its over maturity. Once the cooking process was deemed to have served its purpose, we virtually gorged our selves. What a wonderful feeling, having a full stomach however, the current enjoyment would be short lived. With the onset of gaseous pains, we all retired to our bunks, and those of us who were considered, as juniors and uninitiated, were obviously occupants of the "high rise" bed- chamber!! As such and because the natural phenomena was for gas odour to rise, we found ourselves in an almost untenable situation. However, we had no options, and as such tried to suffer more or less, in silence.

Amid the moans and groans suddenly Blackie Blackmore from Montreal suggested to another multiple years Kriegi, short for Kreigsgefangener, which was German for prisoner of war Red Gordon, from Toronto Islington, "Hey Red let's show these sprogs our little trick". We so called sprogs had no idea what was about to happen. When Red agreed and both he and Blackie got out of their bunks, it was apparent we would soon find out.

The "Jerries" always turned off the power at sundown. This meant the complete camp, with the exception of the guards' searchlights and certain other administration lights, was in a dim, rapidly becoming blackout mode after the power was cut off.

Never-the less, it was still possible to see Red get on the table, on his belly, nude from the waist down. Once so postured, Blackie standing beside the table asked "are you ready Red?" to which Red responded "yep" Blackie struck a match and moved it very close to Red's buttocks, at which time Red cut one. Well let me tell you, a flame approximately two feet long and propane gas in colour seemed to have exploded from Red's buttocks. The response from everyone in the room was to burst out laughing, immediately followed by "do it again Red!"

Although Red was able to successively give us two encores, a third attempt was a disaster, with the smell of burning hair accompanied by painful screams from Red removing any doubt as to the cause. The entertainment now completed, we went back to belly aches and foul odours.

I think most people would agree that the events of this evening, displayed how our Canadian boys, refused to let the enemy destroy their sense of humour even after three years in captivity.

Reid (Red) Gordon, one of my roommates, became my hero. I believe his upbeat manner and sense of humour made daily life bearable. His escape history also earned him great respect from all in our hut.

Red joined up in May of 1940 and began his initial training in Regina July 1, 1940 along with his future brother in law, Don (Pappy) Elliott. Just before his graduation at Brantford,

Ontario, Red flew low over the family home in Islington, Ontario. Someone reported him and as punishment, he, along with numerous others, was not awarded his commission.

Red joined 218 Squadron, Number 3 Group and flew Wellingtons in North Africa. His aircraft was shot down by flak at Bardia, North Africa On August 17, 1941.

Red could speak a little German and when he and his crew were being flown across the Mediterranean to Athens, Greece, he was able to convince the German pilot to let him fly the aircraft for a time.

He was then transported to Germany by train. Red escaped at Marburg on the Austro-Yugoslav border and was captured at Linz some nine days later. He was then sent to the Gestapo prison in Vienna. In November, he was sent to the Prisoner of War Camp at Frankfurt en Main. He again escaped.

As the story goes, he donned the hat and coveralls worn by the goons and had a ladder over his shoulder. When the guard at the gate questioned him, Red, using his German, told him the Commandant wanted him and he had to hurry. He reached the river, stripped down and swam across. He ended up bare-naked in the middle of a German Sunday School picnic. It was back to prison and solitary confinement for three weeks.

Red then was sent to Stalag VIIIB at Lamsdorf, Upper Selesia. That did not deter Red from trying again. In the dead of winter, on Christmas night he and John Snowden, a British Warrant Officer cut through the barbed wire in a heavy snowstorm. He apparently made it all the way to Yenz, on the Czeck border where the Sergeant who had brought him back to camp from the river recognized him.

In March 1942, Red was sent to Stalag Luft III but for some reason was relocated to Stalag Luft VI in East Prussia in June of 1943. It was here, in September, he again escaped and managed to be on the lam for twenty- eight days before being recaptured. As the story goes, Red, apparently very hungry, ate turnips from a farmer's field, developed dysentery and had to turn himself in. Into solitary again!

It was said that Red spent more time in solitary confinement than many of the guys had spent as POWs, a slight exaggeration I suggest.

Red's commission to Officer came through while he was interred in Camp Oflag III and in April 1944, he was moved into our compound at Stalag Luft III.

In 1947, Red received a citation for his efforts while a prisoner of war. An excerpt from the citation reads as follows:

"organized educational and athletic activity among Canadians in POW camps. His efforts secured better receipt of Red Cross parcels, educational material, and a freer flow of mail. He organized classes and lecture groups and was particularly active in promoting athletics. A versatile athlete himself, he captained several baseball and hockey teams."

I also learned through Red's daughter Patti, Gunter Frenzel, the German Air Force officer who allowed Red to fly the plane to Athens and captivity, contacted Red's wife Betty in December 1985. Frenzel sent best wishes by letter to Red and enclosed a picture of him from 1940, dressed in his Luftwaffe uniform. Sadly, Red had passed away the month before. Betty however, wrote back telling him about Red's life, family, interests and his death. All of this had been arranged through a Canada Post mailperson who had committed his time to trying to reconnect Canadians and Germans who had met each other during the war.

It is interesting to note it was Gunter Frenzel who initiated the request to find Red Gordon. In Germany, it had become known that the Canadian Postman was successfully involved in reconnecting WWII veterans.

It would seem that "Dear Red" left lasting impressions with people, even his enemies.

Another example of Kriegi ingenuity was the construction of a theatre. It was explained to the Camp Commandant (CC) that there were a lot of talented actors and directors within the ranks of the camp population. This was intended to plant in the CC's thought process, that if the prisoners as a whole had entertainment, it could conceivably have the tendency of keeping them more occupied, and perhaps less eager to construct escape tunnels. Little did he know that the construction plans for the theatre were such, it was not built like all the other camp billets. Those had a three foot crawl space under the floor, which allowed the Ferrets (regular troops trained to technically "sniff: out escape tunnels) to regularly check for tunnels. Instead the under floor of the theatre was fully boarded in, so that when there was need for extra space to some times hide new excavation sand, as was the case in the Great Escape tunnels, that space served a very useful role. However, the CC and his staff had greatly underestimated the ingenuity and brain trust of our escape artists.

It should be noted that the CC and his senior staff, were always invited to new productions, and they were most enthusiastic about attending.

The tunnel workers were enthusiastic for a different reason. It meant they were able to do their thing, without the usual interruptions from the ferrets. The great escape tunnels were named Tom, Dick and Harry and were at slightly different sites within our compound. They were not intended as triplicates, but rather as backups in the event of the main one being discovered.

The senior officers in charge decided to proceed at once with Harry. This decision was soon over-ruled when it became obvious that a new American compound under construction was ahead of schedule and would be on top of Dick's proposed route. The decision was to put all resources into finishing Tom. The move was an apparent success and Tom was just about complete, when its entrance was accidentally discovered by one of the ferrets. Although this was a real set back, it did take the heat off the workers on Harry, because the Germans had suspected a tunnel was being constructed. Now that they had found one, they never even dreamt that other tunnels might be nearing completion, and they were therefore lulled into a sense of false security, based completely on their discovery of Tom. What had appeared as a disaster a few days ago was now, recognized by the escape committee as a break-through waiting to be exploited.

After a short delay, it was full speed ahead on Harry, and the tunnel was soon completed. March 24 was set as the date for the escape, which once set was irrevocable because of the dates, which had to be on train passes, personal identities and other documents.

The rest is history. Seventy six prisoners got out of the tunnel, which at a planned three hundred and thirty foot distance, proved to be fifteen feet short of reaching the forested area. A German guard on patrol looking for a place to urinate accidentally stepped on the tunnel exit, which resulted in no more escapees and no lead-time for the escapees that had successfully evacuated the tunnel prior to its discovery. If the tunnel exit had been in the forest as planned, or even if the guard had not needed to pee precisely at that particular time, many more would have escaped, and would have had a lead-time of as much as twelve hours.

In any event, of those that initially escaped, only three, reached Sweden, and the remainder were re- captured. Of those, fifty were murdered on Hitler's personal directive to the Gestapo, and the rest were returned to Stalag Luft III.

The Commandant and his Officer Corps were highly annoyed by the execution of the fifty re-captured escapees, and made every effort possible to ensure the Senior British officer, and through him the rest of the camp's prisoners, were advised that the murders were carried out by the Gestapo, and not by the Luftwaffe.

The rumour quickly spread and the various Allied governments directed the POWs, further planned escapes would not be considered advisable, but tunnelling and other escape measures were to continue, thereby ensuring the Jerries did not reduce the number of the military personnel currently required to operate, and provide security for the camp, as well as avoiding the transfer of additional troops to the front lines.

This is where I and other new "Kriegies" came in. There was no doubt that the advancing Allied Armies made for excellent morale among the POWs, and through the camps concealed radios the BBC kept us up to date daily as to where both the Eastern and Western fronts were located.

We made blowtorches using small tins such as British tobacco tins and if they were not readily available, any small tin about the size of a salmon tin would do. The tin must have a tin top into which a small hole is punched at the centre for a cloth wick. We normally used melted oleo margarine for fuel but any other light oil could be used. We would then use a tube (car fuel line) approximately three to four inches long with a diameter about the size of today's' milkshake straw. The tube would be used to blow through the flame, and this would create a very hot blue flame not unlike one from a propane torch. The torch was then used to melt the manufacturers seam on empty bully beef tins. This lead solder was then reused for many other purposes.

The guards, also known as ferrets or goons, were the special guards always present in varying numbers within the compound. Their prime purpose in life was to locate escape tunnels under construction, or any other mysterious activities, before they became functional. They would walk into our rooms anytime they wished.

We in turn had our own security corps of POWs whose main responsibility was to know when and where these ferrets were, at any given time when they were in the compound. This setup started at the nearest barrack to the compound entrance where our security people had a "Duty Pilot" stationed. His responsibility was to log in and out all Luftwaffe personnel during the daylight hours.

Every ferret had a code name provided by our security officers such as, Snoopy, Goofy, Grumpy, etc. It was quite humorous at times. The ferret just coming in to our site or just leaving would go up to our Duty Pilot and say "Grumpy In" or "Goofy Out".

When a ferret entered our room, we would immediately start brewing a small pot of coffee, and the aroma would soon permeate the room.

The Germans were known to be great coffee drinkers and as the war progressed, they were forced by tremendous supply shortages to do without their treasured coffee and use a substitute called ersatz, which in no way resembled real coffee.

The guard would hang around in our room, just enjoying the smell of real coffee and we would pour about half a cup for everyone and noisily enjoy it in front of him. This same scenario would be repeated for this specific guard for at least two more of his visits and then on the third visit, he too would be given a cup. His visits would become more regular and on each occasion, he would be given a cup of beloved coffee.

After approximately three visits of this nature, Red, with his fluent German, would ask him if he could bring us something mundane such as a piece of ruptured inner tube. Generally, the guard would agree and in the next day or so, he would produce the requested item. This was naturally followed up by the cup of coffee as a reward. As the requested items became more valuable, the guard would become increasingly resistant to produce it. Red would then remind him what he had already done, was highly illegal and if this information was passed on to his superior officer, he could be sent to the Russian front or, if it was thought he was aiding and abetting the escape plans of the enemy, he could be executed as a traitor to the Reich. Now he was faced with a dilemma. Ask for a transfer to the front or continue his relationship with us for his small rewards.

The success rate of this type of operation was very high, and extremely productive for the Escape Committee, as they had numerous requirements for all sorts of items needed for fabrication of escape paraphernalia such as uniforms, identification documents, train tickets, leave passes, maps etc. Their brilliance never ceased to amaze all of us in the compound.

I must point out that what might seem to the average person as a cheap cup or two of coffee, or a small piece of chocolate, was valuable to us, as we were always hungry. We relied on our Red Cross parcels for our very existence. These parcels were to provide us with approximately eight to ten pounds of food per week but in 1944, towards the end of the war, our parcels were not arriving as scheduled. As I mentioned before the Allied Air Forces virtual destruction of the German Military Supply system had made the Red Cross Parcel delivery unreliable at best, and in many cases we received a shipment only once a month.

Another example of the fantastic talents available in our camp involved one of our Kriegies, who decided to build a three-foot submarine. He started by bribing guards to get pieces of tin, sufficient in size for the body of the sub and conning tower, a trumpet or other type of brass horn for the valves to be used for engine pistons and other miscellaneous items for the boiler etc. The fuel for the project was melted oleo margarine. I don't remember many of the details, but the finished product cruised around our large fire pond, then suddenly it would submerge for a few minutes. It would then resurface and cruise around the pond for several minutes more. The ingenuity of its designer was fantastic and even the Luftwaffe officers and guards were impressed.

Another example of ingenuity by an inmate was a large mantel style clock constructed from wood alone, no metal of any kind was used.

Again, through bribery links, parts needed for a wireless radio setup were available and we always had our daily BBC news. Only a very few POWs were involved in the process of getting the parts, building the radio, operating it and the security of it. The radio people always had a backup set hidden away, thereby ensuring continuance of our daily news, in the event the ferrets found the one in current use.

At approximately noon each day, the bearer of the news would start his rounds of all the barracks. Simultaneously, our own security people would set up guards at both ends of the barrack or barracks where the news was about to be read. In this way, because of our "Duty Pilot" program, we always knew if any non-residents of our compound were present.

When the news was about to be read in your barracks, upon a given signal, we would all move into the hallway and unless we had a security alert, the news courier would read the BBC news of the day.

Red obtained a map of Europe, which I traced onto a large sheet of paper. After the news was read each day, I would plot the Allied advances. The German news as a general rule, unless favourable to the German cause, was at least three to four days later and sometimes longer, than what I had plotted on the map. This resulted in the Ferrets coming to Red, and asking why I was always so much ahead of their own news releases. Red responded, "He reads the stars."

Gambling was another way of passing the days. I remember one Kriegie losing about one hundred dollars playing backgammon. He recovered his money by pushing a ping-pong ball with his nose, around the full perimeter of the camp.

We could write cheques on anything to pay off gambling debts or purchase food, cigarettes and other items from fellow prisoners. Those who made it back were actually able to cash them at the banks, as long as the Bank's name and address, and the inmates account number were printed on them and of course the inmate's signature.

Although POWs would save various goodies out of their Red Cross parcels for bartering with the guards, they could and would also sell or trade items with their fellow prisoners. Naturally, the price reflected the availability, which was obviously wholly dependent on if and when parcels arrived on site. The current situation since the allied landings and the Russian advances, uncovered vast supplies of parcels hoarded by veteran Kriegies who had wisely put them aside for situations such as those currently developing.

The purchase of a ham & cheese sandwich on German black bread from a Kriegie could cost you up to $35.00 or more. To buy a real bar of chocolate could be as high as $50.00, and a can of coffee might fetch as much as $100.00. Inflationary prices, you bet.

CHAPTER EIGHTEEN
THE HORROR MARCH

It was obvious from the daily news reports, the Russians on the East and the British, American and Canadian forces on the West were steadily advancing on all fronts. Our future, if there was such an animal, was open to speculation. There were those who believed we would not be moved and that the Russians would eventually overrun and hopefully, one way or another return us to Britain. About this time, Hitler supposedly made it known that Germany's many thousands of Allied Prisoners of War, would as a last resort, be used as bargaining tools with the Allies. This theory was obviously most disconcerting to all of us, however with the next rumour that we were about to be moved out and headed west, the supposed Hitler plan appeared to have merit. In the meantime, as directed by our SBO (Senior British Officer) we were advised to devise sleds, carriages and good old fashioned back packs, to carry food, clothing, blankets and anything else deemed necessary for our survival, bearing in mind your ability to transport it. Our bed boards were a most desirable "in demand" item.

On January 25 and 26, our news stated that the advancing Russian military had crossed the Oder River which was approximately fifty miles from Stalag Luft III. The excitement amongst the POW populace was fantastic, even though we were still uncertain as to our own immediate future. In any event, most of us felt the odds favoured us moving west.

The SBO and his staff once more emphasized that we fabricate whatever we could in the way of sleds or backpacks to assist us in moving our essentials. Bed slats, boxes, and whatever else we could find were quickly assembled as sleds and loaded up with food, blankets, and anything else we thought to be crucial to our survival. Despite the rather overwhelming excitement at what would be a completely new adventure, and hopefully the end of our imprisonment there was a lingering doubt, as to our ability to survive in the severe winter weather currently embracing our area. In particular, one must recognize that our clothing was hopelessly inadequate. We had no such thing as gloves, winter boots, earflaps, or parkas. I think the vast majority of us were still wearing some portion of the gear we had on when shot down. Needless- to- say there were exceptions to the norm because of trading parcels from home in the earlier years, and scrounging from the guards. The lack of gloves was perhaps the worst problem, although we solved this in most cases by using extra socks.

Somewhere close to midnight on January 27 1945, the goons and their dogs herded us from our now unheated barracks into the yard and formed us into columns. The temperature was around minus thirty degrees centigrade. We set out onto roads covered with five or six inches of snow, with very strong winds blowing hard enough to provide, what those of us from the Prairie Provinces in Canada would describe as a blizzard.

It should be appreciated that we did not have any type of vehicular transport for hauling food and other necessities, and therefore the extra time waiting to leave resulted in many prisoners adding to the sled and pack loads they had already deemed adequate. They would no doubt in most cases, discover in the very near future, the error of their ways.

The number of prisoners from Stalag Luft III was about ten thousand. Most of, if not all the Allied prisoners held west of Berlin were evacuated westbound like ourselves, although in most cases, by different routes. The estimated and generally accepted number of total POWs from all services was estimated at two hundred and fifty thousand. Of these, an estimated twenty five thousand or ten percent would perish on the March. I certainly do not know where this figure came from, its validity, or by whom it was made. In any event, the March had begun. Where were we going? No one knew at this time. The speculators were many in numbers and certainly varied in their opinions on where our final destination would be. What we all did know was that the temperature was very cold, the wind was blowing very hard, we were walking in approximately five to six inches of snow, and it was still snowing.

It did not take long before problems began to develop for a large number of our group. Their sleds were giving up the ghost, largely due to poor construction. They now faced the dilemma of abandoning a large part of their goodies or finding another way of transporting them. In most cases, they had no choice but to abandon many of the items they had so carefully selected. A large numbers of Red Cross parcels had to be left on the side of the road. What a loss.

The first village we passed through was approximately fifteen kilometres from Stalag Luft III. I cannot remember its name, but suffice to say it was of no importance to us other than our escorts allowed us a fifteen-minute rest break. This was used to readjust our loads and for most, to answer natures call. The number one item still of primary importance to us was keeping warm. Stopping early in our travel only resulted in us getting cold again.

After a very short so-called rest period, we began walking again and as time passed, we began looking forward to stopping for a period of rest. Even though the Geneva Convention specified how often and how long these rest periods were to be, our Senior British Officer (SBO) more often than not, dictated when, where and for how long. The Luftwaffe Commandant usually approved this, and particularly more so as the distance travelled increased.

Our next stop was supposed to be in a large town called Friewaldau, a further fifteen kilometres where we were to spend the night. The last few kilometres before the town resulted in many more sled breakdowns, necessitating further abandonment of food parcels. There were many cases of POWs collapsing, resulting in their being loaded onto wagons bringing up the tail end of our column. We had no idea of the numbers of those who ended up on the wagons, but at the end of our trip, we, could not account for about five hundred POWs. I have never heard that number substantiated.

When we arrived in Friewaldau, the town was crawling with refugees, mostly German civilians fleeing the rapidly advancing Russian armies. There was absolutely no covered accommodation available for us and standing in the well below freezing temperature was absolutely intolerable. A decision was quickly made and we continued on to Lieppe, approximately seven more kilometres.

Upon arrival, the first groups of six or seven hundred were, almost immediately put up in barns. Our group, of approximately the same number, had to wait nearly four hours in minus twenty-five degree centigrade temperature, and double digit wind speeds, before we were able to find similar accommodations. By this time, we had been on the road for approximately fifteen hours, and had only travelled about thirty-six kilometres. While not a world record, given the terrible conditions under which we had been forced to travel, we deemed it to be, a fair accomplishment.

The barn, we were housed in had lots of freshly unbundled hay with its wonderful aroma. We quickly lied down and being totally exhausted, almost at once fell asleep.

It was extremely crowded but this was really a bonus as the closeness of our bodies actually provided sufficient heat to make the temperature tolerable. These almost satisfactory conditions, our standards being very low at this stage, were unfortunately cursed by the overwhelming stench of vomit and feces from the numerous kriegies, who for fear of losing their bed, had defecated in their clothing. In spite of this, most of us fell asleep very quickly, some not even removing their boots as many of them had frozen feet. Regardless of the disadvantages, this was better than slowly freezing to death.

At around 0800 hours, on January 30th, we were once again on the road. It was considerably warmer and having had a good night's sleep, we were in a much better frame of mind.

Once again, we were speculating as to what the future had in store for us. Information from our leaders suggested we were heading for Marlag Milag Nord, an abandoned German Naval barracks not too far from Bremen.

We travelled approximately twenty kilometres and finally after about ten hours, reached a fair sized town called Muskau, which appeared to have lots of available accommodation. There, we found shelter in a large glass manufacturing plant.

After having a very basic bit of one of our Red Cross food parcels, we all went to sleep and had our first good rest, which included most of the next day. We were ordered out shortly after the sun went down on February 1st.

I must take a few moments to mention the reception we generally received from the German civilian population while on this march. It was a very pleasant surprise indeed.

On numerous occasions, many of the German citizens, who lined the streets of the villages and towns we passed through on our trek gave us milk, bread, and sometimes vegetables. On one occasion, an older woman brought out a pitcher of warm milk. One of the most miserable members of our guards said her act was "verboten" and emphasized this by pushing her back with his rifle. She defied him to shoot her and pushed right back until he relented and backed off. She gave numerous of our boys the hot milk. Red, my Canadian roommate from Luft III, said she had screamed at the guard that her son was a POW in Canada and the Canadians were treating him very well.

I'm certain the guards, most of whom were at least fifty years old, realized the outcome of the war was overwhelmingly in our favour and as a rule, they were reasonable in any of the dealings our group had with them.

The trip today started out very well. The weather was much warmer and most of the snow was disappearing. We still had to be careful as much of the road had icy patches, the result of melting during the day and re-freezing as the temperature dropped after the sun went down.

We had only travelled a few kilometres before I started feeling increasing soreness in my right foot. Before too long, the same soreness started in my left foot. At the first rest stop, I took off my boots and to my dismay, discovered both feet had been bleeding quite badly and now my socks were stuck to my feet. My only recourse was to put my boots back on and hope for the best, or ask the guards to put me on one of the wagons bringing up the rear. This I quickly ruled out as I would have to separate from my own comrades and only God knew if I would ever reunite with them.

At around two or three in the afternoon, we arrived at Spremburg, where they told us we would be travelling most of the remaining distance to Marlag Milag by train. This was certainly good news for me as the pain in my feet appeared to be lessening but numbness was quickly replacing it.

The guards provided us with some drinking water, long overdue, but certainly well received. In my case, this meant I could remove my boots, and soak my feet until I could remove my socks with less effort. It was only now I realized the cause of my problem occurred at the glass factory the night before. I along with several others had slept beside a large bin, containing extra fine sand, apparently used for the final sanding of glass panes. We had taken our boots off for comfort while we slept. Minute amounts of this sand found their way into our socks, and while walking, had virtually sanded the skin off our poor old feet. Now they tell us! One of the chaps had some gauze and Red, talked one of the guards into getting some ointment for my feet. Fortunately, I had extra socks, which along with the fact we would be riding for several days, gave me a real break.

It would take almost three years after my return to Canada before my feet stopped peeling.

It was finally time to load the railway boxcars, as we called them in Canada. Each car was supposed to hold forty men or eight horses. Well they loaded at least fifty and likely closer to sixty men and their equipment into our boxcar. Even worse was the fact the boxcar itself still contained both human and animal feces, and the stench was absolutely unbearable. In fact, it resulted in many of our group and up until now healthy cohorts, vomiting as well.

After cramming in the human cargo, it became obvious that the car was in no way capable of seating much less laying down the number of Kriegies on board.

As far as ventilation facilities, the car had four ports, one in the top of each corner, each approximately ten inches lengthwise and five inches deep. We were rather fortunate that the German authorities started the train moving very quickly after the guards closed and locked the doors from the outside. As a result, we did not have to suffer from the oppressive heat and stench one could imagine would accompany with doors closed and cars at a standstill.

I do not want to dwell on the terrible conditions to which we were subjected for the next forty-eight hours. Suffice it to say, the stench of feces, vomit, and other unidentified foul smelling filth were incomprehensible.

We used milk powder cans for pee cans but when a user tried to throw the contents out of one of the ventilation inlets while the train was moving at high speed, well no doubt you know the result. "Shower anyone?"

Before long and despite the terrible odours, just about everyone slumped to the floor, completely fatigued, in what I can best describe, as a state of unconsciousness.

The morning of February 3 brought us back to reality as those of us who were fortunate enough not to have dysentery or diarrhoea were again facing the horrible state of chaos that surrounded us. Although we might not be personally suffering from the foregoing maladies, it was almost impossible to avoid gagging or vomiting because of the unimaginable stench we had to breathe in from the surrounding atmosphere. I think this was undoubtedly the worst situation I have ever experienced.

The Germans told us we would finally have food supplied in an upcoming railway station called Halle. This turned out not to be true as another train, hospital I think, had beaten us to the punch. We would be one more day without food. I suspect this may have had some value for those too sick to eat, but for the rest of us it only meant that we had nothing to vomit up, which may have been a blessing in disguise.

We reached Hanover on the morning of February 4, where we got off the train. That was wonderful! I found it rather humorous as well. As I looked up and down the railway tracks, all I saw was a line of white bottoms, as hundreds tried to take advantage of an opportunity to relieve themselves.

We got our first bit of drinking water in nearly two days, from whatever source we could find. Being on the outskirts of the railway station, this meant civilian houses. Although numerous people refused to open their doors, many more did so. You can imagine their reaction when they saw all these dirty and extremely smelly men. It is hard to believe how most people we approached seemed to be in sympathy with us, and when we requested water in our limited German, "Vasser bitte" they would hurriedly get some for us. Maybe they were just glad to get rid of us and if so, who could blame them.

That same evening, we reached our next stop, Tarmstedt. Once again, we were able to leave the foul smelling boxcars and once again breathe without gagging. We then had only a few kilometres to walk, which was almost a blessing in disguise.

When we reached the barracks at Marlag Milag, the guards forced us to stand in heavy rain for several more hours while they searched us. Surely, they did not consider us a threat to the Homeland security. In any event, the rain was in some aspects well received as a poor man's shower, and helped in some small way to dispel some of the odours and filth that resulted from the train ride.

Finally somewhere around midnight or later on February 5, we were able to enter our new barracks. They had been unoccupied for some time but to us tired miserable old Kriegies they were somewhat like a Hilton hotel. There were bunks available in our room, but most if not all of us chose to sleep on the straw strewn floor. When morning came, many of our roommates said they had experienced rats running over them during the night. I along with many others did not share that experience or maybe we were just too exhausted to notice.

CHAPTER NINETEEN
MARLAG MILAG NORD, BREMEN

The quarters that became our lodging for the next sixty days had been a prison camp for allied merchant seamen in the past, but obviously had been vacant for a long time and were in terrible condition. The current resident rat population was well established and very reluctant to share or give up their tenancy. After the hell we had gone through since leaving Stalag Luft III, this accommodation appeared to us as if we were lodged in a first class hotel. For a large number of our companions suffering from exhaustion, dysentery, frost- bite, and other maladies, it provided a haven for their recovery, although a significant number had to be hospitalized, just where, we were not certain. The Luftwaffe authorities assured us they were being well looked after.

Although we normally were not permitted to travel off the base, some small groups, under escort, were given permission to scavenge for firewood, and they, with their tales upon their return, made the rest of us extremely jealous.

The time seemed to pass very quickly. I suspect it was the fact most if not all of us were more washed out than we thought. The healing process due to the lack of food and more importantly nourishing food was bound to take considerably more time than normal for those suffering from any medical problems. My twenty -second birthday came and went.

We were very fortunate to have our clandestine radio back on line very quickly after our arrival. This was primarily due to the expertise of our radio personnel and by the almost non-existent security searches by our goons. We therefore had our daily news courtesy of the BBC, which kept us up to date on the great advances the Allies were making on all fronts.

Finally, we could actually hear the Allied bombardments to the south of us and we were not surprised when the guards ordered us out of the camp late in the day on April 9. For reasons unknown to us, we returned to our quarters shortly thereafter, and did not depart again until the next morning.

Our Senior British Officer was Group Captain Wray of the Royal Canadian Air Force, who was later my Air Officer Commanding when I served in Europe during the Cold War in 1960-63. That however, is another story.

CHAPTER TWENTY
LUBECK

Our march, en route to Lubeck was at the most, snail speed, about one mile per hour, with numerous rest stops. The guards now were almost like companions rather than the enemy. On one occasion, friendly aircraft dropped leaflets featuring a senior German officer standing on the gallows. The message below the picture stated that he had mistreated Allied POWs and was about to be executed. Apparently Group Captain Wray showed this to the Luftwaffe Colonel with the admonition that this would be his fate if he did anything considered as maltreatment of Allied POWs. The threat was obviously well taken by the Colonel and from that point on, it appeared Group Captain Wray was "calling the shots."

We had one particularly bad incident occur on day three of this leg of our trek. Two RAF ground attack Typhoons circled us and then the lead aircraft commenced an attack. As he dived at us, the vast majority, if not all, had taken cover, as per normal routine. A Naval officer stood in the centre of the road, waving frantically at the obviously attacking aircraft. The attacker's first volley tore off the officer's legs, killing him and two of his naval comrades. From that point on, if any aircraft came into our area, everyone, and I mean everyone took cover in the ditches or in many cases, the L shaped trenches along the roadside.

My own experience on two occasions when I dove into one of the trenches, I landed on top of a guard. They no doubt were much older than I was, but obviously, more experienced at diving into roadside trenches.

I can remember the Russian prisoners marching in the opposite direction from us, looking starved and bedraggled, and their faces covered in sores and I remember we shared some of our meagre food with them. We felt sorry for them despite our own problems. Obviously, their treatment was far worse than ours was.

The march was now almost slow enough to be more like a stroll. Many Kriegies began mixing with the German residents along the way, begging, borrowing, and yes on occasions, stealing any available items of food. In most cases, the excess coffee and cigarettes most of us had brought with us, proved to be extremely valuable "trade items." They were definitely very highly desired by most of the German populace who had been without real coffee for many months.

On the 29 of April, we finally arrived at a large and lavish Estate at Trenthorst, only a few kilometres from Lubeck. The story quickly spread that the owner himself, had been a POW and had only recently, been repatriated from North America, where he said the treatment they received was first class. He was very pleased he now had the opportunity to reciprocate.

Most of us occupied large well-maintained barns, and most importantly, we had access to water and hoses to remove the accumulated filth from our bodies. What a wonderful feeling.

Apparently upon arrival at this large and extremely well kept estate, Group Captain Wray had emphatically directed the Luftwaffe Commandant, that we were to remain at the Estate rather than proceed into Lubeck, which was already "bursting at the seams" with multi national POWs and civilian refugees. More importantly, there were reports that a large segment of the population was infected with numerous deadly and highly contagious diseases. With the increasing sounds of heavy artillery, accompanied by almost continuous overhead flights of Allied aircraft, the Luftwaffe Commandant was in no position to deny our SBO's demands. In fact, we already had many German military personnel giving us their weapons, and reversing their position from guards to becoming our prisoners. They no doubt felt it was a wise decision on their part.

We settled down in our new "home away from home" in one of the larger barns, complete with ample amounts of new sweet smelling hay. Heaven on Earth best describes our new situation. The rumble of heavy artillery nearing us from the southwest was music to our ears.

With dusk quickly approaching, Ludvig Domanski a Polish pilot, asked me if I would like to accompany him down to the foreign workers' quarters, only a short distance from our current site. Having lucked in on so many dangerous situations in my almost immediate past, I was not about to be shot on a venture that I would consider to be of little value, other than curiosity. After much cajoling on Ludwig's part, I reluctantly agreed.

Shortly after darkness fell, Ludwig led the way, quietly navigating past several non- existent guard posts to a military type barracks. We soon arrived at a unit housing the Russian foreign workers' foreman and his lovely wife. Ludwig, who spoke fluent Russian, introduced me to the couple from whom we received huge warm and sincere hugs.

Ivan, (honestly, that was his name) was well over six feet tall and I would guess an extremely well built two hundred pounds. His wife on the other hand was a beautiful blonde about five feet two inches and perhaps one hundred and fifteen pounds. Oh, what a wonderful hug that was! After a brief conversation, repeated back to me in English, Ludvig momentarily left me on my own with Ivan and his beautiful wife. Naturally, the conversation, if you could call it that, slowed to a crawl because of our individual linguistic inabilities. The whole situation was not only boring, but also extremely tiring, which was evident by the numerous yawns from both sides.

During one of the breaks in our attempts to converse, Ivan pointed at me followed by a faked yawn and clasping of both hands to form an artificial pillow for his head. I quickly nodded agreement with him. His next sign language was to point at me and then point to their bed. He then indicated he and his wife would sleep on the floor. I by nodding my head sideways and uttering nein nein made him understand that I would not and could not do that. He then followed up with more sign language, by pointing to his wife and me and the bed, followed by pointing to him-self and the floor. The message was obvious and though very tempting, also very shocking. My immediate response was to shake my head negatively and at the same time loudly and often repeat "Nein, nein!" Ivan's reaction was to scream at me loudly in Russian accompanied by threatening me with his fists. Fortunately, for me, Ludwig heard Ivan shouting and realizing I was in deep trouble, returned quickly to my rescue.

Stepping between us, he spoke in Russian and asked Ivan why he was so angry with me. Ivan quickly responded and as he continued his dissertation, Ludwig started smiling. Grasping Ivan by the shoulders, he responded in Russian. Ivan by his facial expressions was obviously very puzzled. As Ludwig continued, Ivan's face lit up and he suddenly started laughing, as did his beautiful bride. He then grabbed me, gave me a huge bear hug, and kissed me on both cheeks. I was very relieved, to say the least, but still perplexed as to why all this had occurred. Ludwig quickly explained, when Ivan offered me the opportunity to sleep with his wife, by refusing, I had not only insulted him, but more importantly, I had insulted his beautiful wife. Ludvig explained to them, that this was not acceptable in our society, but now that I understood the Russian meaning, I was very honoured by their gesture. Ivan's response was that our society must be stupid.

I was almost recaptured when an American in the RCAF, whom I had met on the march, rescued an abandoned car? and the two us went on a joy ride. A British Recce unit intercepted us, and their Lieutenant informed us we must have ended up behind the German lines without realizing it; somehow, we got back to the safe zone without incident. I guess LADY LUCK was on my side again.

CHAPTER TWENTY-ONE
LIBERATION AND HOME

On May 2, 1945, the 11th British Armoured Division rolled into Lubeck and we knew we were now, really free. Their mobile Medical Unit obviously was aware of the thousands of Allied POWs for whom they were now responsible. For the next forty-eight hours, it seemed like every time we turned around, they were subjecting us to another de-lousing. On the third day, they issued new clothing that included Army Battle dress, and a small amount of cash, about five hundred francs, which was very much appreciated.

Within a few days, we flew to Brussels, where we received briefings not unlike those we would have given our teen-age children, under similar circumstances. The briefings also included the pick up points and times for the next forty-eight hours, in which the transport vehicles would take us back to the airport and on to Britain.

The ride down town was very exciting to say the least. As we rode in the back of the Army stake trucks taking us to more or less the centre of the city, it was apparent that the word had spread through the various media, informing the public of our identity. Wall to wall people, welcoming us back to civilization, lined the streets. Because of the massive crowds, our transport trucks travelled at a very slow pace, which allowed what I estimated as thousands of girls, to pull many of our Kriegis out of the trucks, with little or no apparent objections. On one occasion, a young (pretty I am sure) lady, got a death hold on the front of my blouse. She almost hauled me out, but some of my so-called buddies would not let her win the tug of war. I sure gave them hell afterward.

Later on in the evening, after visiting numerous Pubs where I do not think any of us were charged for our drinks, I will always remember, walking arm in arm through the streets singing Brabanconne, the Belgian National Anthem. Wow what a reception! What a night! What a wonderful memory!

We flew back to #3 PRC (Personnel Reception Centre) in Bournemouth where we were under medical supervision for about two or three weeks. We had to eat every two hours as our stomachs had shrunk from lack of food. I was in fairly good shape having lost only about fifteen to twenty pounds while others had lost forty- five and fifty pounds or more. I am certain to this day, it was my small size that allowed me to survive as well as I did on the March.

While in Bournemouth, I remember drinking a bottle of Scotch every day but I could not get drunk. I got so concerned about it, that I went to the Military Doctor at the Centre, and after having a few chuckles, he told me not to worry, I would get drunk in due course. It was just my nerves feeding on the alcohol, and it was a common occurrence among ex POWs. His theory became reality about two weeks later. Good thing, because the Scotch was costing about sixty dollars a bottle due to its popularity, and all the extraordinary parties going on all over the British Isles.

During this time in England, I received a telegram from John, my Flight engineer asking me to come on up to Preston. I had also written a letter to Mr. and Mrs. Archibald, Archie's mom and dad and received a telegram from them shortly thereafter, asking me to come to Garmouth. I did not do either.

I do not really know why, but none of the ex POWs were being allowed any leave, at least not until the Medical Staff was confident there were no medical problems still undiagnosed. Perhaps it was the painful memory of our last operation. Perhaps I felt guilty for not protecting Archie, their only son as I had promised; perhaps I had not done enough to ensure my crew could get out of the aircraft. Perhaps perhaps, perhaps? These thoughts would haunt me for many years to come, and during my incarceration, I discovered with the many discussions I had with other aircraft Captains, that it was quite a normal reaction.

Shortly after the Medical people gave me the OK to travel, they booked me on the Louis Pasteur, a French ocean liner. along with the several hundred Canadian Army ex POWs the Germans had taken prisoner after the debacle at Dieppe. They were still so bitter about the heavy loss of life, and the impossible task given to them, especially, when every day air reconnaissance could or would, obviously have shown the mass build up by the German troops, and their prime entrenchment in bunkers on the cliffs above the beaches.

To pass the time, some of the Army boys started several crap games in the passenger lounge, which quickly became very popular. In my case, I had unfortunately developed an ulcerated tooth, which created personal agony, and with no Dentist on board, the gambling to some degree seemed to get my mind off the pain.

On the third or fourth day, the ship's Captain arrived on the scene, and after demanding our attention, advised us that he would not tolerate gambling on his ship, and further more, the lounge would be out of bounds to all of us if we did not obey his orders. If I were to state that his ego had obviously kidnapped his brain, I think all present would agree with me. However, the show was just starting.

A very large mean looking Senior NCO walked up to the Captain and towering over the "gentleman" jabbed his finger into the Captain's chest. In a loud growl he said, "Sir I suggest you leave this lounge immediately and do not return until such time as we disembark from YOUR ship, Failure to do so will result in you having one hell of a long swim." I guess the Captain decided discretion was the better part of valour, and we never saw him in the lounge again; come to think of it, I never saw the Senior NCO again either.

After docking in Montreal, we were bunked in the Lachine military camp for several days while the Medics gave us medical examinations, and in my case removed my ulcerated tooth. I then proceeded by train west bound, arriving in Winnipeg on 12 June 1945. Now I really felt like I was home. I bid goodbye to the Army boys, many of whose company I enjoyed whilst listening to their stories. I too felt much healthier as my poor old mouth had more or less healed after the tooth extraction in Montreal.

Winnipeg was more or less the pivotal point for those of us from Western Canada, and for those of us who had signed on for the Japanese conflict. In the latter case, there was some re- kitting requirements, plus some extra administrative paper work. This also included a disembarkation leave pass, plus a pay parade and a reporting date (TBA) for those of us who had volunteered for the Eastern Front. My date was on conclusion of my leave, and I was to report to the RCAF Holding Unit in Dauphin Manitoba. Now the Welcome Home Party can begin.

About ten or twelve of us decided to start at a well-recommended Steak House with a barbecued steak and lobster dinner accompanied by several bottles of wine, thoroughly enjoyed by most if not all of us. Prior to heading back to barracks, I visited the latrine while one member of our group was phoning for a couple of cabs. In a few minutes, one of our guys opened the door to advise me that the cabs were waiting; I quickly joined our gang for the trip back to our temporary home. That quickness later proved to be a very expensive few minutes. The next morning when I more or less recovered from my worst hangover in several years, I suddenly realized that the very expensive and personally engraved Bulova watch Mom and Dad had given me prior to my leaving for Britain, was nowhere to be found. I called the Steak House but no one had turned my watch in. I rushed off down town to a Birks jewellery store, and after telling them my sad story, which included my having to leave for home this evening, they in a wonderful gesture, hand engraved an almost identical Bulova watch at a price well below that ticketed. When I sincerely thanked them, they responded, "no it is we who want to thank you, for what you have done for all of us."

Prior to leaving that early evening, I phoned Mom and Dad to tell them my arrival time in Swift Current. I could almost swim out of that phone booth because of the accumulated tears from both parties. Is this realism or am I dreaming? After talking to my loved ones in Tuberose, I called my Grand Parents and my Aunt Louise in Moose Jaw, telling them our estimated arrival time. More tears and kisses. I recalled my leaving Moose Jaw for Europe almost three years ago, and on that day as the train pulled out, I definitely remember as clearly as if it was yesterday, my Grand Parents and Aunty sobbing and waving good bye, and my wondering, will I ever see them again,

As we rolled into the Depot in Swift Current, my heart was pounding at a speed a Doctor would normally consider dangerous. Suddenly, I spotted my whole family waving frantically as we came to a full stop. Even as fast as I was de- training with the assistance of the train's Conductor, my brothers and sister were already at the bottom of the stairs taking my bags as I came down. Dad was supporting Mom as I virtually flew into their arms, everybody was crying as we hugged and kissed. This had to be the greatest day in my life. My mother looked wonderful to me, although more frail than when I last saw her, in what seemed like decades ago. Dad did not look any different, but my brothers and sister are the ones that had changed the most.

Later on while we were having lunch, Mom suddenly said, "Two nights ago I dreamt you had lost your watch". Although I was surprised, I must have really expected as much, as I nonchalantly held out my left arm complete with "suspect" Bulova, with the accompanying comment, "you mean this one mom?"

Upon his return home, Al learned that while a prisoner of war, he had been awarded the Distinguished Flying Cross on November 4, 1944. The citation read as follows:

Flight Lieutenant Trotter has participated in numerous attacks over heavily defended targets in Germany and enemy occupied territory. Throughout he has displayed fine leadership and has

pressed home each attack with the greatest determination, often in the face of the heaviest opposition. This officer's outstanding skill and keenness for operational flying have set a fine example to all.

EPILOGUE

Upon returning to Canada from Europe in 1945, I volunteered to serve in the Pacific Theatre. Based at Paulsen Manitoba awaiting assignment, the war with Japan ended and I received an honourable discharge from the R.C.A.F. on October 5, 1945.

I returned to the farm, but found myself so hyperactive, I could not settle down to every day life. In 1946, I, along with nine others took three self -propelled combines, three grain trucks, and a refuelling truck south of the border to Montgomery Alabama where we combined flax. We worked all the way back to Saskatchewan, combining wheat. This trip helped me to settle down somewhat and I was able to achieve a significant amount of normality to my life.

I then registered at the University of Saskatchewan and was accepted into their pre-law curriculum. While waiting for commencement, I spent a year as a fireman with the Canadian National Railway for the sole purpose of earning money for University. This proved unattainable in that I missed flying so badly, I spent almost all my earnings renting aircraft.

In 1948, six weeks prior to commencement of University, I received a request from the R.C.A.F. to return to the R.C.A.F. as a short service (five years) commissioned officer with the rank of Flying Officer. I accepted by return wire.

This was a stopgap measure by the R.C.A.F. to ensure they had adequate experience in the Service to see them through the period of waiting for military trained University graduates.

On September 1, 1948, I reported to 435 Squadron in Edmonton, Alberta. The squadron's main role was the re-supply of the northern stations located in Fort St. John, Fort Nelson, Watson Lake, and Whitehorse. I also flew regular flights to the arctic bases in Kittyguzuit, and Cambridge Bay, and often on the weekends, conducted parachute training for the Princess Patricia Canadian Light Infantry.

In early 1949, I met my future wife, Valerie Collins, a pretty and young flight attendant employed with Canadian Pacific Airlines. Although relatively few short service commissioned officers received Permanent Commissions, through determination and other attributes, I was finally granted my much desired the P C.

From Edmonton, I was transferred to Montreal. Our #1 daughter Leslie, co-author of this book and most importantly #1 "Daddy Pusher" to ensure completion of Against the Odds, arrived by stork in Edmonton. No daddy. Poor Mom did a first class job with no assistance from Dad.

My job at the time was Chief Instructor of the Air Transport Command Operational Training Unit for all aircrew trades on C47, North Star, C119 and C45 aircraft. Val and Leslie joined me in Montreal however, I was only there for three months before leaving them to assume the role of Commanding Officer, Resolute Bay, in the Arctic. While there, I supervised the multi million-dollar reconstruction projects on base, which was located fifteen hundred miles north of Churchill, Manitoba. The closest tree was fifteen hundred miles south of our base. The construction was completed in six months and I returned to Montreal.

From there I went to 426 Squadron, which was a long-range transport unit, which supplied Resolute Bay and other Arctic stations. I made regular scheduled flights to the United Kingdom and spent nearly two years flying transport support for the Korean War. In addition, on one trip, I transported Canadian Special Forces to Viet Nam. On this mission, I carried on the trip around the world in a mere twenty days. Due to prevailing winds, it was quicker to continue around the world than fly the direct route home.

I then continued in the position of Staff Officer Plans and subsequently Staff Officer Operations at Air Transport Command Headquarters.

After graduating R.C.A.F. Senior Officer Staff College, I FINALLY got my wish to become a fighter pilot. After graduation from the Operational Training Unit at Cold Lake, Alberta, I was posted to #445 CF100 All Weather Jet Fighter Squadron in Marville, France, as the Commanding Officer.

The squadron was on twenty-four hour alert three hundred and sixty five days of the year during the Cold War.

All four CF100 Squadrons were closed down in 1963 and I was transferred to #1 Advanced Flying School, Gimli, Manitoba as Commanding Officer of the Basic Training School (sixty Tudor jets) and the Advanced School (16 T33 Jets) Here we trained fighter pilots not only from Canada, but from around the world. Graduates from the Advanced School received their pilot's wings.

While at Gimli, I was invited to visit Cold Lake, Alberta by the Commanding Officer of the CF104 Squadron. There I managed several flights on the CF104 Super Sonic Fighter, on which, I had the pleasure of exceeding twice the speed of sound, fourteen hundred miles per hour, at an altitude of fifty thousand feet. I also received my Mach II pin for this accomplishment.

After four years as Commanding Officer at #1 AFS, I was subsequently transferred to the position of Commanding Officer of the Air Defence Radar Station in Kamloops, British Columbia. After two and a half years there and a total of twenty-six years serving my country, I elected to take early retirement and I took my final leave. Now I could truly enjoy, full time, my wonderful wife and our six great kids.

After leaving the Air Force I designed nine golf courses and supervised the construction of six

I had a fantastic career in the Royal Canadian Air Force and other than the two hundred and sixty eight days spent as a Prisoner of War, I thoroughly enjoyed every moment.

Even the POW experience taught me a lot about myself and the incidentals we too often take for granted.

Thank you, Leslie for pushing me into telling my stories. If it had not been for you, my memoirs never would have been published.

Thank you Val, for putting up with me for sixty years and providing me with a great family of three sons and three beautiful daughters.

Upon retiring in 1969, Lieutenant Colonel Trotter had over 10,000 hours of flying on the following aircraft:

DH 82
Cessna
Oxford
Whitley
Halifax   -four-engine bomber
Lancaster-four-engine bomber
Anson
C45-twin-engine light transport
C47-DC 3 and Dakota
North Star-four-engine transport-flew around world in 20 days
Goose-small flying boat
C119-heavy-duty troop carrier twin engine
T 33-training jet
Tudor-training jet
CF 100 all weather twin engine jet fighter
Comet   transport aircraft
C5-deluxe transport for VIPs
F104- Super Sonic Fighter Jet-Exceeded twice the Speed of sound

Lt. Colonel Trotter holds the following Decorations
Distinguished Flying Cross
Distinguished Flying Medal
1939 -45 Star
Aircrew Europe and France Germany Star and Clasp
Defence Medal
Canadian Voluntary Service Medal with Bar
War Medal

Special Service Medal Korea

Special Service Medal with N.A.T.O. Bar (Cold War 3years Europe)

Canadian Peace Keeping Service Medal (Israel-Egyptian War)

United Nations Medal for Korea

Centennial Medal – 1967

Canadian Forces Service Medal and Clasp

Today, Lt. Colonel Trotter is 86 years old, and lives in Kamloops, British Columbia with his wife of 59 years Val. They have three sons, Jack Daniel and Robert, three daughters, Leslie, Laurie, Valerie, and eight grandchildren, Cassie, Michelle, Andrew, Robert, Joel, Nicole, Evan and Sam. He is an avid golfer, playing a full18 holes of golf twice or three times per week. He continues to speak at schools and Business clubs in the Kamloops area every year in honour and remembrance of our Veterans of all wars.

LIST OF SORTIES FLOWN

101 Squadron

November 18, 1943-Berlin
November 22, 1943-Berlin
November 23, 1943-Berlin (Aborted)
November 26, 1943-Stuttgart
December 02, 1943-Berlin
December 03,1943-Leipzi (Aborted)

156 Squadron

January 07, 1943	Stettin
	Aborted
	Instruments U/S
January 20, 1944	Berlin
	Early returns
	Navigator passed out
January 21, 1944	Magdeburg
January 27, 1944	Berlin
January 28, 1944	Berlin
February 15, 1944	Frankfurt
February 19, 1944	Leipzig
February 20, 1944	Stuttgart
February 24, 1944	Schweinfurt
March 15, 1944	Stuttgart
March 18, 1944	Frankfurt
March 22, 1944	Frankfurt
March 24, 1944	Berlin
March 30, 1944	Nurnberg

582 Squadron

| April 24, 1944 | Karlsruhe |
| April 27, 1944 | Freiderichshaven |

May 07, 1944	Nantes
May 11, 1944	Louvaine
May 19, 1944	Boulogne
May 22, 1944	Dortmund
May 27, 1944	Rennes
June 06, 1944	Cherbourg to LeHavre
June 15, 1944	Douai
June 23, 1944	Coubronne
June 24, 1944	Middelstraete
June 28, 1944	Oisemont – Neuville
June 28, 1944	Blaineville Sur Lea
June 30, 1944	Villers Bocage
July 02, 1944	Oisemont-Neuville
July 06, 1944	Coquereur
July 09, 1944	L'Hey
July 10, 1944	Nucourt
July 11, 1944	Gapenne
July 12, 1944	Rollez
July 15, 1944	Ducourt
July 18, 1944	Cagny
July 18, 1944	Vaires
July 20, 1944	Ferme de Forestol
August 10, 1944	Dijon
August 12, 1944	Russelsheim (Missing)

PUBLISHED SOURCES

156 Squadron Website

Bomber Command Diaries – Martin Middlebrook

Lie in the Dark and Listen – Ken Rees

The Last Escape- John Nichol and TonyRennel

Master Bombers – Sean Feast

OFFICIAL RECORDS

Air 27/801/802

Air 27/802/804

Air 27/1041/1042

Air 27/2051/2054

R.C.A.F. military records of Elmer John Trotter